Bonjour et  to "3 Minute Fren based in the UK, a /ou to learn to spe.

This book contains "Course 5" of the 3 Minute French series. The methodology will get you speaking quickly, without the struggle normally associated with language learning.

I'll not bore you with my life story or intricate details of the history of the methodology; I know you probably just want to start learning French now, so I'll let you get on with it.

Actually, I've changed my mind, I will bore you a little before we start. It's my book! I'll keep it as brief as I can though.

I've been tutoring people for over ten years on a one-to-one basis in a range of subjects. I love languages, I love learning and I love teaching. I also love chocolate, but this isn't really the place to discuss my chocoholism. I'm very lucky that I get to teach people every day. However, I can't fit everybody who asks me into my schedule so, regrettably, I end up turning a lot of people away. I wish I could teach the whole world but I'm yet to figure out a way of duplicating myself!

The next best thing is to teach through the medium of a book. So, that's what I've decided to do. If you're reading this book, then I will soon be teaching you the glorious splendour that is the French language.

Anyway, I'll stop blathering on in a minute and we'll get started with learning. But, firstly, let me just say this...

Hullabaloo!

No, I'm joking, of course, let me say this instead...

We are all human beings, which means we all possess the attributes that make us human beings. There's a wonderful quote by a man called Terence:

"I am human, and nothing that is human is alien to me"

What it means is that if one person is capable of something, then we are all capable of it, because we're all humans too. There's nothing in the world that I cannot understand if somebody before me has succeeded in understanding it. Therefore, it's only logical that since there are more than 200 million people in the world who have managed to learn to speak French, then you can learn it too!

Anyway, philosophising over. Let's begin.

3 MINUTE FRENCH

COURSE 5

LESSONS 36 – 44

KIERAN BALL

Visit my website or follow me on Facebook, Twitter or Instagram for more language hints and tips:

www.3minute.club
www.twitter.com/3mlanguages
www.facebook.com/3minutelanguages
www.instagram.com/3minutelanguages

Contents

LESSON 36

Let's start this lesson with a quick recap of the words and phrases we learnt in the last lesson. How do you say the following in French?

I've hurt my...
I've broken my...
some medicine
I've caught
a cold
the flu
I feel
I don't feel
ill

If there are any words you can't remember, go back to the last lesson and have a quick review of them before you start this lesson. It's really important that you remember the words you've learnt so far before you move on to learn any more.

Let's pick a verb as the first word for this lesson:

acheter

It means "(to) buy"
You pronounce it "ash-TAY"

WORD LIST SO FAR

acheter – *(to) buy*

How would you ask this in French?

What do you want to buy?

What can I buy?

I would like to buy that.

I'm going to buy that tomorrow.

What do you want to buy?
Que voulez-vous acheter?

What can I buy?
Que puis-je acheter?

I would like to buy that.
Je voudrais acheter ça.

I'm going to buy that tomorrow.
Je vais acheter ça demain.

How would you ask this in French?

What are you going to buy for Marie?

I'm going to buy a bottle of wine for Pierre and Marie.

I would like to buy dinner for you tonight.

I'm going to buy a coat.

What are you going to buy for
Marie?
**Qu'allez-vous acheter pour
Marie?**

I'm going to buy a bottle of wine
for Pierre and Marie.
**Je vais acheter une bouteille de
vin pour Pierre et Marie.**

I would like to buy dinner for you
tonight.
**Je voudrais acheter le dîner pour
vous ce soir.**

I'm going to buy a coat.
Je vais acheter un manteau.

If you put a little "le" in front of "acheter" then you get this:

l'acheter

It means "(to) buy it"
You pronounce it "lash-TAY"

WORD LIST SO FAR

acheter – *(to) buy*
l'acheter – *(to) buy it*

How would you say these sentences in French?

I would like to buy it.

Do you want to buy it?

I'm going to buy it for Pierre tomorrow.

Can I buy it for you?

When are you going to buy it?

Where are you going to buy it?

I would like to buy it.
Je voudrais l'acheter.

Do you want to buy it?
Voulez-vous l'acheter?

I'm going to buy it for Pierre tomorrow.
Je vais l'acheter pour Pierre demain.

Can I buy it for you?
Puis-je l'acheter pour vous?

When are you going to buy it?
Quand allez-vous l'acheter?

Where are you going to buy it?
Où allez-vous l'acheter?

Here's your next word in French:

cher

It means "expensive"
You pronounce it "share"

WORD LIST SO FAR

acheter – *(to) buy*
l'acheter – *(to) buy it*
cher – *expensive*

How would you say these sentences in French?

It's very expensive.

I would like to buy it but it's too expensive.

It's too expensive for me.

It isn't expensive.

It's very expensive.
C'est très cher.

I would like to buy it but it's too expensive.
Je voudrais l'acheter mais c'est trop cher.

It's too expensive for me.
C'est trop cher pour moi.

It isn't expensive.
Ce n'est pas cher.

How would you say these sentences in French?

I would like to hire a car but it's very expensive.

I would like to eat here but it's too expensive for me.

I think it's too expensive.

I would like to hire a car but it's very expensive.
Je voudrais louer une voiture mais c'est très cher.

I would like to eat here but it's too expensive for me.
Je voudrais manger ici mais c'est trop cher pour moi.

I think it's too expensive.
Pour moi, c'est trop cher.

Here's a useful word in French:

quelque chose

It means "something"
You pronounce it "kel-keugh-SHOZE"

WORD LIST SO FAR

acheter – *(to) buy*
l'acheter – *(to) buy it*
cher – *expensive*
quelque chose – *something*

So, how would you say these sentences in French?

I have something for you.

Can you buy something for Pierre?

I would like to buy something here.

I would like to buy something here for Marie but everything is too expensive.

I have something for you.
J'ai quelque chose pour vous.

Can you buy something for Pierre?
Pouvez-vous acheter quelque chose pour Pierre?

I would like to buy something here.
Je voudrais acheter quelque chose ici.

I would like to buy something here for Marie but everything is too expensive.
Je voudrais acheter quelque chose ici pour Marie mais tout est trop cher.

And, how would you say these sentences in French?

Do you have something for me?

Are you going to buy something for Pierre?

Can you buy something for me?

Do you have something for me?
Avez-vous quelque chose pour moi?

Are you going to buy something for Pierre?
Allez-vous acheter quelque chose pour Pierre?

Can you buy something for me?
Pouvez-vous acheter quelque chose pour moi?

Here's a useful thing to buy if you're ever on holiday:

une carte postale

It means "a postcard"
You pronounce it "oon kart poss-TAL"

WORD LIST SO FAR

acheter – *(to) buy*
l'acheter – *(to) buy it*
cher – *expensive*
quelque chose – *something*
une carte postale – *a postcard*
des timbres – *some stamps / any stamps*

How would you say these sentences in French?

Where can I buy a postcard?

Do you have any postcards?

The postcards here are very beautiful.

How much is a postcard?

I would like a postcard from Paris.

Where can I buy a postcard?

Où puis-je acheter une carte postale?

Do you have any postcards?

Avez-vous des cartes postales?

The postcards here are very beautiful.

Les cartes postales ici sont très belles.

How much is a postcard?

C'est combien une carte postale?

I would like a postcard from Paris.

Je voudrais une carte postale de Paris.

How would you say these sentences in French?

I'm going to buy a postcard.

Are you going to buy a postcard from Marseille for me?

The postcard is from Marie.

I'm not going to buy a postcard.

I'm going to buy a postcard.
Je vais acheter une carte postale.

Are you going to buy a postcard
from Marseille for me?
**Allez-vous acheter une carte
postale de Marseille pour moi?**

The postcard is from Marie.
La carte postale est de Marie.

I'm not going to buy a postcard.
**Je ne vais pas acheter une carte
postale.**

You'll need these if you want to post your "carte postale":

des timbres

It means "some stamps" or "any stamps"
You pronounce it "day TAM-breugh"

WORD LIST SO FAR

acheter – *(to) buy*
l'acheter – *(to) buy it*
cher – *expensive*
quelque chose – *something*
une carte postale – *a postcard*
des timbres – *some stamps / any stamps*

How would you ask this in French?

Do you have any stamps?

I would like to buy four stamps, please.

Do you have any stamps?
Avez-vous des timbres?

I would like to buy four stamps, please.
Je voudrais acheter quatre timbres, s'il vous plaît.

How would you say this in French? Just remember that you can change the word "des", which means some/any, to "les", which means "the".

Where are the stamps?

Where are the stamps?
Où sont les timbres?

How would you say these sentences in French?

I'm going to buy some stamps for my postcard.

How much is it for three stamps?

The stamps are here.

Where can I buy some stamps?

I would like three stamps.

I'm going to buy some stamps for my postcard.
Je vais acheter des timbres pour ma carte postale.

How much is it for three stamps?
C'est combien pour trois timbres?

The stamps are here.
Les timbres sont ici.

Where can I buy some stamps?
Où puis-je acheter des timbres?

I would like three stamps.
Je voudrais trois timbres.

This word is identical in French and English:

un souvenir

It means "a souvenir"
You pronounce it "an(g) soo-veugh-NEER"

WORD LIST SO FAR

acheter – *(to) buy*
l'acheter – *(to) buy it*
cher – *expensive*
quelque chose – *something*
une carte postale – *a postcard*
des timbres – *some stamps / any stamps*
un souvenir – *a souvenir*
ma mère – *my mum*

How would you say these sentences in French?

Where can I buy a souvenir?

I would like to buy a souvenir for Marie.

I'm going to buy a souvenir from La Rochelle.

The souvenirs here are very expensive.

Where can I buy a souvenir?

Où puis-je acheter un souvenir?

I would like to buy a souvenir for Marie.

Je voudrais acheter un souvenir pour Marie.

I'm going to buy a souvenir from La Rochelle.

Je vais acheter un souvenir de La Rochelle.

The souvenirs here are very expensive.

Les souvenirs ici sont très chers.

How would you say these sentences in French?

How much is a souvenir?

Where are the souvenirs?

Are you going to get a souvenir for me?

Do you have any souvenirs?

How much is a souvenir?
C'est combien un souvenir?

Where are the souvenirs?
Où sont les souvenirs?

Are you going to get a souvenir for me?
Allez-vous acheter un souvenir pour moi?

Do you have any souvenirs?
Avez-vous des souvenirs?

Now this last phrase is somebody you might like to buy a souvenir for:

ma mère

It means "my mum"
You pronounce it "mah mair"

WORD LIST SO FAR

acheter – *(to) buy*
l'acheter – *(to) buy it*
cher – *expensive*
quelque chose – *something*
une carte postale – *a postcard*
des timbres – *some stamps / any stamps*
un souvenir – *a souvenir*
ma mère – *my mum*

So, how would you say these sentences in French?

I would like to buy a souvenir for my mum.

Where is my mum?

I would like to buy a souvenir for my mum.
Je voudrais acheter un souvenir pour ma mère.

Where is my mum?
Où est ma mère?

Family members

I've put a vocabulary expansion section at the end of this book with a list of family members in French. If it's a masculine family member, the word for "my" will be "mon". If it's a feminine family member, the word for "my" will be "ma". If it's more than one family member (e.g. my parents) the word for "my" will be "mes".

WORD LIST SO FAR

acheter – *(to) buy*
l'acheter – *(to) buy it*
cher – *expensive*
quelque chose – *something*
une carte postale – *a postcard*
des timbres – *some stamps / any stamps*
un souvenir – *a souvenir*
ma mère – *my mum*

How would you say these sentences in French?

My mum is here tomorrow.

I have ordered a pizza for my mum.

I have something for my mum but she isn't here.

My mum is in France.

My mum is here tomorrow.
Ma mère est ici demain.

I have ordered a pizza for my mum.
J'ai commandé une pizza pour ma mère.

I have something for my mum but she isn't here.
J'ai quelque chose pour ma mère mais elle n'est pas ici.

My mum is in France.
Ma mère est en France.

How would you say these sentences in French?

I'm going to have dinner with my mum tonight.

My mum is here.

My mum isn't here.

I'm going to have dinner with my mum tonight.
Je vais prendre le dîner avec ma mère ce soir.

My mum is here.
Ma mère est ici.

My mum isn't here.
Ma mère n'est pas ici.

WORD LIST SO FAR

acheter – *(to) buy*
l'acheter – *(to) buy it*
cher – *expensive*
quelque chose – *something*
une carte postale – *a postcard*
des timbres – *some stamps / any stamps*
un souvenir – *a souvenir*
ma mère – *my mum*

It's time to practise what we've learnt in this lesson.

Grab a piece of paper and see if you can write down the following sentences in French. Then, you can check the answers.

1. I would like to buy something for my wife
2. I have something for my daughter
3. I'm going to buy something for my dad
4. Do you have any stamps?
5. How much is a postcard?
6. I'd like to buy something here for my sister, but everything is too expensive for me
7. Can I buy some stamps, please?
8. I have something for my mum
9. Can I buy a postcard here?
10. I'm going to buy a souvenir for my friend

1. Je voudrais acheter quelque chose pour ma femme
2. J'ai quelque chose pour ma fille
3. Je vais acheter quelque chose pour mon père
4. Avez-vous des timbres?
5. C'est combien une carte postale?
6. Je voudrais acheter quelque chose ici pour ma sœur, mais tout est trop cher pour moi
7. Puis-je acheter des timbres, s'il vous plaît?
8. J'ai quelque chose pour ma mère
9. Puis-je acheter une carte postale ici?
10. Je vais acheter un souvenir pour mon ami

Now, let's have a go at doing some reverse translations. Again, write down the English translations of the following French sentences, then check to see if you were correct.

1. Où puis-je acheter une carte postale?
2. Où puis-je acheter un souvenir?
3. J'ai quelque chose pour Pierre
4. Ça c'est trop cher
5. Je voudrais l'acheter pour mes grands-parents
6. Voulez-vous acheter quelque chose ici?
7. J'ai quelque chose pour mon cousin
8. C'est trop cher pour moi
9. Je voudrais acheter ce manteau rouge
10. Pour moi, c'est absolument trop cher

1. Where can I buy a postcard?
2. Where can I buy a souvenir?
3. I have something for Pierre
4. That is too expensive
5. I would like to buy it for my grandparents
6. Do you want to buy something here?
7. I have something for my cousin
8. It's too expensive for me
9. I would like to buy this red coat
10. I think it's absolutely too expensive

What we're going to do now are some recap translations, which will incorporate words we learnt in the previous lesson.

1. I'd like the same thing as Pierre
2. Are you going to the hotel?
3. What do you want to eat?
4. I've broken my toe
5. I'm going to order now
6. What are you going to drink?
7. Are you going to do the same thing as me?
8. I've got a stomach ache
9. I'm not tired
10. Are you going to have lunch here?

1. Je voudrais la même chose que Pierre
2. Allez-vous à l'hôtel?
3. Que voulez-vous manger?
4. Je me suis cassé l'orteil
5. Je vais commander maintenant
6. Qu'allez-vous boire?
7. Allez-vous faire la même chose que moi?
8. J'ai mal à l'estomac
9. Je ne suis pas fatigué
10. Allez-vous prendre le déjeuner ici?

Let's now do some French to English recap translations. Grab a piece of paper and see if you can work out what these sentences mean.

1. Pouvez-vous acheter du fromage à l'aéroport?
2. Où était Pierre hier?
3. Où voulez-vous prendre le dîner plus tard?
4. Je vais au restaurant
5. Puis-je manger ça?
6. Que voulez-vous boire?
7. Je vais appeler Marie
8. Je vais à Marseille demain
9. Êtes-vous pressé?
10. J'ai mal à la main

1. Can you buy some cheese at the airport?
2. Where was Pierre yesterday?
3. Where do you want to have dinner later?
4. I'm going to the restaurant
5. Can I eat that?
6. What do you want to drink?
7. I'm going to call Marie
8. I'm going to Marseille tomorrow
9. Are you in a hurry?
10. I've hurt my hand

Let's recap all the words we've learnt so far. How did you say these words in French?

1. I've hurt my...
2. if it's possible
3. I'm going
4. she is
5. a cold
6. it was
7. I have
8. (to) make/do it
9. (to) buy
10. I ordered
11. is he?
12. in a hurry
13. the same thing as Pierre
14. some stamps / any stamps
15. how
16. the same thing as me
17. what
18. I don't feel
19. is she?
20. expensive
21. do you want?
22. some/any medicine
23. today
24. how are you?
25. (to) eat
26. another (a different type)
27. now
28. I'm not
29. I have reserved / I have booked
30. in the name of
31. I feel
32. the same thing as you
33. was
34. something
35. it wasn't
36. Mr
37. tired
38. the same thing as her
39. she isn't
40. (to) order
41. I'm not going
42. the same thing as him
43. I am
44. (to) try it
45. ill
46. the same thing

47. I'm doing well
48. Mrs
49. are you?
50. I'm called
51. I ate / I've eaten
52. a souvenir
53. (to) change
54. I've caught
55. the flu
56. later
57. he is
58. busy
59. Miss
60. (to) buy it

61. I've broken my...
62. (to) drink
63. another (the same type) / again
64. my mum
65. are you going?
66. yesterday
67. a postcard
68. (to) change it
69. wasn't
70. for you
71. he isn't
72. fine / well

1. j'ai mal à...
2. si c'est possible
3. je vais
4. elle est
5. un rhume
6. c'était
7. j'ai
8. le faire
9. acheter
10. j'ai commandé
11. est-il?
12. pressé
13. la même chose que Pierre
14. des timbres
15. comment
16. la même chose que moi
17. que
18. je ne me sens pas
19. est-elle?
20. cher
21. voulez-vous?
22. un médicament
23. aujourd'hui
24. comment allez-vous?
25. manger
26. un/une autre
27. maintenant
28. je ne suis pas
29. j'ai réservé
30. sous le nom de
31. je me sens
32. la même chose que vous
33. était
34. quelque chose
35. ce n'était pas
36. monsieur (M.)
37. fatigué
38. la même chose qu'elle
39. elle n'est pas
40. commander
41. je ne vais pas
42. la même chose que lui
43. Je suis
44. l'essayer
45. malade
46. la même chose
47. je vais bien
48. madame (Mme.)
49. êtes-vous?
50. je m'appelle

51. j'ai mangé
52. un souvenir
53. changer
54. j'ai attrapé
55. la grippe
56. plus tard
57. il est
58. occupé
59. mademoiselle (Mlle)
60. l'acheter
61. je me suis cassé...

62. boire
63. encore
64. ma mère
65. allez-vous?
66. hier
67. une carte postale
68. le changer
69. n'était pas
70. pour vous
71. il n'est pas
72. bien

LESSON 37

Let's start this lesson with a quick recap of the words and phrases we learnt in the last lesson. How do you say the following in French?

(to) buy
(to) buy it
expensive
something
a postcard
some stamps
a souvenir
my mum

If there are any words you can't remember, go back to the last lesson and have a quick review of them before you start this lesson. It's really important that you remember the words you've learnt so far before you move on to learn any more.

Now, we've already learnt this word:

quelque chose

It means "something"
You pronounce it "kel-keugh-SHOZE"

WORD LIST SO FAR

quelque – *something*

How would you say these sentences in French?

I would like to eat something.

Are you going to buy something?

Can I have something?

I would like to eat something.
Je voudrais manger quelque chose.

Are you going to buy something?
Allez-vous acheter quelque chose?

Can I have something?
Puis-je avoir quelque chose?

Well, let's add a little extra to the end of it:

quelque chose de la région

It means "something from the region"
You pronounce it "kel-keugh-SHOZE deugh lah ray-JSHON(g)"

WORD LIST SO FAR

quelque chose de la région – *something from the region*

So, how would you say these sentences in French?

I would like something from the region.

Where can I buy something from the region?

I'm going to buy something from the region for Sophie.

Do you want something from the region?

Are you going to buy something from the region?

I would like something from the region.
Je voudrais quelque chose de la région.

Where can I buy something from the region?
Où puis-je acheter quelque chose de la région?

I'm going to buy something from the region for Sophie.
Je vais acheter quelque chose de la région pour Sophie.

Do you want something from the region?
Voulez-vous quelque chose de la région?

Are you going to buy something from the region?
Allez-vous acheter quelque chose de la région?

You can take the "de la région" part and put it onto other things too:

de la région

It means "from the region"
You pronounce it "deugh lah ray-JSHON(g)"

WORD LIST SO FAR

quelque chose de la région – *something from the region*
de la région – *from the region*

So, how would you say these sentences in French?

I would like to try some wine from the region.

Do you have any cheese from the region?

It's from the region of Provence.

What are you going to buy from the region?

I would like a souvenir from the region.

I would like to try some wine from the region.
Je voudrais essayer du vin de la région.

Do you have any cheese from the region?
Avez-vous du fromage de la région?

It's from the region of Provence.
C'est de la région de Provence.

What are you going to buy from the region?
Qu'allez-vous acheter de la région?

I would like a souvenir from the region.
Je voudrais un souvenir de la région.

You can put any adjective on the end of "quelque chose" with the help of the little word "de":

quelque chose de + adjective

It means "something + adjective"

Something tasty

So, in French, if you want to say "something tasty", you have to put a "de" after the word for "something" and before the word for "tasty". So, what you're literally saying is "something of tasty".

quelque chose de délicieux
something tasty

quelque chose de bon
something good

quelque chose d'extraordinaire
something extraordinary

How would you say these sentences in French?

I would like something tasty.
(delicious)

I would like to try something different. *(différent)*

Where can I buy something expensive?

I would like something tasty.
(delicious)
Je voudrais quelque chose de délicieux.

I would like to try something different. *(différent)*
Je voudrais essayer quelque chose de différent.

Where can I buy something expensive?
Où puis-je acheter quelque chose de cher?

How would you say these sentences in French?

I've caught something terrible.

I have something good for you.

Do you want something small?

I've caught something terrible.
J'ai attrapé quelque chose de terrible.

I have something good for you.
J'ai quelque chose de bon pour vous.

Do you want something small?
Voulez-vous quelque chose de petit?

Here's your last phrase for this lesson:

quelque chose de français

It means "something French"
You pronounce it "kell-keugh-SHOZE deugh fron-SAY"

WORD LIST SO FAR

quelque chose de la région – *something from the region*

quelque chose de + adjective – *something + adjective*

quelque chose de bon – *something good*

quelque chose de français – *something French*

How would you say these sentences in French?

Can I try something French today?

I'm going to order something French.

I would like to eat something French.

Can I try something French today?
Puis-je essayer quelque chose de français aujourd'hui?

I'm going to order something French.
Je vais commander quelque chose de français.

I would like to eat something French.
Je voudrais manger quelque chose de français.

How would you say these sentences in French?

I ordered something French, not a pizza.

I would like something French.

Are you going to have something French? *(food)*

I ordered something French, not a pizza.
J'ai commandé quelque chose de français, non pas une pizza.

I would like something French.
Je voudrais quelque chose de français.

Are you going to have something French? *(food)*
Allez-vous prendre quelque chose de français?

WORD LIST SO FAR

quelque chose de la région – *something from the region*

quelque chose de + adjective – *something + adjective*

quelque chose de bon – *something good*

quelque chose de français – *something French*

It's time to practise what we've learnt in this lesson.

1. It's something fantastic
2. I'm not going to eat something French today; I would like a pizza
3. I would like to buy something from the region for my family
4. Do you want to eat something French?
5. I would like to buy something good, but everything's too expensive
6. I ordered something French, not a pizza!
7. I would like to try something French today
8. What are you going to try from the region?
9. Where can I eat something delicious?
10. I ate something French yesterday

1. C'est quelque chose de fantastique
2. Je ne vais pas manger quelque chose de français aujourd'hui; je voudrais une pizza
3. Je voudrais acheter quelque chose de la région pour ma famille
4. Voulez-vous manger quelque chose de français?
5. Je voudrais acheter quelque chose de bon, mais tout est trop cher
6. J'ai commandé quelque chose de français, non pas une pizza!
7. Je voudrais essayer quelque chose de français aujourd'hui
8. Qu'allez-vous essayer de la région?
9. Où puis-je manger quelque chose de délicieux?
10. J'ai mangé quelque chose de français hier

Now, let's have a go at doing some reverse translations. Again, write down the English translations of the following French sentences, then check to see if you were correct.

1. Voulez-vous acheter quelque chose de la région?
2. J'ai attrapé quelque chose de terrible
3. Je vais commander quelque chose de français
4. Que puis-je acheter de la région?
5. Je vais acheter quelque chose de fantastique pour ma mère
6. Je ne vais pas acheter quelque chose de très cher
7. Je voudrais quelque chose de plus grand
8. Avez-vous quelque chose de plus petit?
9. Où puis-je acheter un souvenir de la région?
10. Allez-vous acheter un souvenir de la région?

1. Do you want to buy something from the region?
2. I caught something terrible
3. I'm going to order something French
4. What can I buy from the region?
5. I'm going to buy something fantastic for my mum
6. I'm not going to buy something very expensive
7. I would like something bigger
8. Do you have something smaller?
9. Where can I buy a souvenir from the region?
10. Are you going to buy a souvenir from the region?

What we're going to do now are some recap translations, which will incorporate words we learnt in the previous lessons.

1. I'm going to the beach at 3 o'clock
2. I've hurt my foot
3. Which car can you hire?
4. I would like to make a reservation
5. Are you going to pay the bill?
6. Where are you?
7. What do you want to do at Marie's house?
8. I'm not going to the beach; I'm too tired
9. I'm not going to Pierre's house; I'm too busy
10. I've hurt my leg

1. Je vais à la plage à trois heures
2. J'ai mal au pied
3. Quelle voiture pouvez-vous louer?
4. Je voudrais faire une réservation
5. Allez-vous payer l'addition?
6. Où êtes-vous?
7. Que voulez-vous faire chez Marie?
8. Je ne vais pas à la plage; je suis trop fatigué
9. Je ne vais pas chez Pierre; je suis trop occupé
10. J'ai mal à la jambe

Let's now do some French to English recap translations. Grab a piece of paper and see if you can work out what these sentences mean.

1. Allez-vous commander le vin?
2. À quelle heure voulez-vous manger?
3. J'ai un café pour vous ici
4. Je ne suis pas ici demain
5. Voulez-vous boire la même chose que moi?
6. La réservation est sous le nom de Smith
7. Pierre n'est pas là
8. J'ai commandé pour Pierre
9. J'ai mal à l'estomac
10. Puis-je manger ça?

1. Are you going to order the wine?
2. What time do you want to eat?
3. I have a coffee for you here
4. I'm not here tomorrow
5. Do you want to drink the same thing as me?
6. The reservation is under the name of Smith
7. Pierre isn't there
8. I've ordered for Pierre
9. I've got stomach ache
10. Can I eat that?

Let's recap all the words we've learnt so far. How did you say these words in French?

1. the same thing as her
2. how
3. (to) buy it
4. I'm going
5. the same thing as me
6. I've hurt my...
7. busy
8. I'm not going
9. it wasn't
10. (to) change
11. for you
12. what
13. a souvenir
14. he isn't
15. (to) change it
16. (to) eat
17. (to) try it
18. something from the region
19. some/any medicine
20. something good
21. expensive
22. something
23. yesterday
24. I ordered
25. tired
26. it was
27. something + adjective
28. fine / well
29. a cold
30. the same thing as you
31. the flu
32. another (a different type)
33. are you?
34. (to) drink
35. now
36. (to) make/do it
37. he is
38. Mrs
39. she isn't
40. I don't feel
41. how are you?
42. is she?
43. my mum
44. I've caught
45. the same thing as Pierre
46. I have
47. the same thing as him
48. in a hurry
49. wasn't
50. another (the same type) / again

51. I'm doing well
52. some stamps / any stamps
53. I have reserved / I have booked
54. something French
55. later
56. if it's possible
57. Miss
58. do you want?
59. I'm not
60. in the name of
61. the same thing
62. I am
63. is he?
64. Mr
65. a postcard
66. I feel
67. was
68. I'm called
69. she is
70. (to) order
71. I've broken my...
72. today
73. ill
74. (to) buy
75. I ate / I've eaten
76. are you going?

1. la même chose qu'elle
2. comment
3. l'acheter
4. je vais
5. la même chose que moi
6. j'ai mal à...
7. occupé
8. je ne vais pas
9. ce n'était pas
10. changer
11. pour vous
12. que
13. un souvenir
14. il n'est pas
15. le changer
16. manger
17. l'essayer
18. quelque chose de la région
19. un médicament
20. quelque chose de bon
21. cher
22. quelque chose
23. hier
24. j'ai commandé
25. fatigué
26. c'était
27. quelque chose de + adjective
28. bien
29. un rhume
30. la même chose que vous
31. la grippe
32. un/une autre
33. êtes-vous?
34. boire
35. maintenant
36. le faire
37. il est
38. madame (Mme.)
39. elle n'est pas
40. je ne me sens pas
41. comment allez-vous?
42. est-elle?
43. ma mère
44. j'ai attrapé
45. la même chose que Pierre
46. j'ai
47. la même chose que lui
48. pressé
49. n'était pas
50. encore
51. je vais bien
52. des timbres
53. j'ai réservé
54. quelque chose de français
55. plus tard
56. si c'est possible

57. mademoiselle (Mlle)
58. voulez-vous?
59. je ne suis pas
60. sous le nom de
61. la même chose
62. Je suis
63. est-il?
64. monsieur (M.)
65. une carte postale
66. je me sens

67. était
68. je m'appelle
69. elle est
70. commander
71. je me suis cassé...
72. aujourd'hui
73. malade
74. acheter
75. j'ai mangé
76. allez-vous?

LESSON 38

Let's start this lesson with a quick recap of the words and phrases we learnt in the last lesson. How do you say the following in French?

something
something from the region
something + adjective
something French

If there are any words you can't remember, go back to the last lesson and have a quick review of them before you start this lesson. It's really important that you remember the words you've learnt so far before you move on to learn any more.

Here's a useful phrase you'll hear quite a lot in France:

il y a

It means "there is" or "there are"
You pronounce it "ee-lee-YAH"

WORD LIST SO FAR

il y a – *there is / there are*

How would you say these sentences in French?

There is a postcard here.

There is a good restaurant here.

There is a supermarket there.

There is a postcard here.
Il y a une carte postale ici.

There is a good restaurant here.
Il y a un bon restaurant ici.

There is a supermarket there.
Il y a un supermarché là.

How would you say these sentences in French?

There is something very beautiful here.

I'm not going to eat here at the hotel tonight; there is a restaurant straight ahead where the food is delicious.

There is a restaurant at the hotel.

There is something very beautiful here.

Il y a quelque chose de très beau ici.

I'm not going to eat here at the hotel tonight; there is a restaurant straight ahead where the food is delicious.

Je ne vais pas manger ici à l'hôtel ce soir; il y a un restaurant tout droit où la nourriture est délicieuse.

There is a restaurant at the hotel.

Il y a un restaurant à l'hôtel.

We can turn "il y a" into a question quite easily:

y a-t-il?

It means "is there" or "are there"
You pronounce it "ee-ah-TEEL"

WORD LIST SO FAR

il y a – *there is / there are*
y a-t-il? – *is there? / are there?*

How would you say these sentences in French?

Is there a hotel here?

Is there a supermarket here?

What is there?

Is there something for me?

Are there any stamps?

Is there a hotel here?
Y a-t-il un hôtel ici?

Is there a supermarket here?
Y a-t-il un supermarché ici?

What is there?
Qu'y a-t-il?

Is there something for me?
Y a-t-il quelque chose pour moi?

Are there any stamps?
Y a-t-il des timbres?

Here's your next phrase in French for this lesson:

près d'ici

It means "near here"
You pronounce it "preh dee-SEE"

WORD LIST SO FAR

il y a – *there is / there are*
y a-t-il? – *is there? / are there?*
près d'ici – *near here*

How would you say these sentences in French?

It's near here.

The hotel is very near here.

It isn't near here.

Is there a restaurant near here?

There is a supermarket near here.

What is there near here?

The carpark isn't near here.

It's near here.
C'est près d'ici.

The hotel is very near here.
L'hôtel est très près d'ici.

It isn't near here.
Ce n'est pas près d'ici.

Is there a restaurant near here?
Y a-t-il un restaurant près d'ici?

There is a supermarket near here.
Il y a un supermarché près d'ici.

What is there near here?
Qu'y a-t-il près d'ici?

The carpark isn't near here.
Le parking n'est pas près d'ici.

Here's another verb to add to your collection:

voir

It means "(to) see"
You pronounce it "vwar"

WORD LIST SO FAR

il y a – *there is / there are*
y a-t-il? – *is there? / are there?*
près d'ici – *near here*
voir – *(to) see*

How would you say these sentences in French?

Can I see the menu, please?

I'm going to see it.

Can I see it?

Are you going to see Marie tomorrow?

Can I see the menu, please?
Puis-je voir le menu, s'il vous plaît?

I'm going to see it.
Je vais le voir.

Can I see it?
Puis-je le voir?

Are you going to see Marie tomorrow?
Allez-vous voir Marie demain?

How would you say these sentences in French?

What time are you going to see Pierre?

I'm not going to see it.

Are you going to see the Eiffel Tower in Paris?

What time are you going to see
Pierre?
À quelle heure allez-vous voir
Pierre?

I'm not going to see it.
Je ne vais pas le voir.

Are you going to see the Eiffel
Tower in Paris?
Allez-vous voir la Tour Eiffel à
Paris?

WORD LIST SO FAR

il y a – *there is / there are*
y a-t-il? – *is there? / are there?*
près d'ici – *near here*
voir – *(to) see*

It's time to practise what we've learnt in this lesson.

Grab a piece of paper and see if you can write down the following sentences in French. Then, you can check the answers.

1. What do you want to see at the town centre?
2. There is a restaurant at the hotel, but it isn't very good
3. Is there a car park near here?
4. Is there a book shop near here?
5. Is there a good restaurant near here?
6. There is a restaurant there
7. There's a postcard for you here
8. There are too many people here today
9. What are you going to see today?
10. What can I see here?

1. Que voulez-vous voir au centre-ville?
2. Il y a un restaurant à l'hôtel mais ce n'est pas très bon
3. Y a-t-il un parking près d'ici?
4. Y a-t-il une librairie près d'ici?
5. Y a-t-il un bon restaurant près d'ici?
6. Il y a un restaurant là
7. Il y a une carte postale pour vous ici
8. Il y a trop de personnes ici aujourd'hui
9. Qu'allez-vous voir aujourd'hui?
10. Que puis-je voir ici?

Now, let's have a go at doing some reverse translations. Again, write down the English translations of the following French sentences, then check to see if you were correct.

1. Il y a un restaurant à l'hôtel
2. Je ne peux pas voir le restaurant
3. Le restaurant est très près d'ici
4. Il y a un restaurant tout droit
5. Il y a un bon restaurant là
6. Y a-t-il une bibliothèque près d'ici?
7. Je vais voir cela demain
8. Je ne peux pas le voir
9. Pouvez-vous le voir?
10. Que pouvez-vous voir?

1. There's a restaurant at the hotel
2. I can't see the restaurant
3. The restaurant is very near here
4. There's a restaurant straight on
5. There's a good restaurant there
6. Is there a library near here?
7. I'm going to see that tomorrow
8. I can't see it
9. Can you see it?
10. What can you see?

What we're going to do now are some recap translations, which will incorporate words we learnt in the previous lessons.

1. I ate here yesterday and it was fantastic
2. I've hurt my mouth
3. I'm going to try some cheese
4. Can you order a pizza for me, please?
5. Yes, she is there
6. When are you going to pay the bill?
7. How much was the car?
8. I'm not going to have dinner
9. I've broken my arm
10. I would like to buy it

1. J'ai mangé ici hier et c'était fantastique
2. J'ai mal à la bouche
3. Je vais essayer du fromage
4. Pouvez-vous commander une pizza pour moi, s'il vous plaît?
5. Oui, elle est là
6. Quand allez-vous payer l'addition?
7. C'était combien la voiture?
8. Je ne vais pas prendre le dîner
9. Je me suis cassé le bras
10. Je voudrais l'acheter

Let's now do some French to English recap translations. Grab a piece of paper and see if you can work out what these sentences mean.

1. Je vais manger maintenant
2. Elle est au restaurant
3. Allez-vous à l'hôtel?
4. Allez-vous faire la même chose qu'hier?
5. Allez-vous commander un café?
6. Voulez-vous un café?
7. Je vais commander la même chose que Pierre
8. Puis-je payer plus tard?
9. Puis-je changer ma réservation?
10. Je vais à Marseille maintenant

1. I'm going to eat now
2. She is at the restaurant
3. Are you going to the hotel?
4. Are you going to do the same thing as yesterday?
5. Are you going to order a coffee?
6. Do you want a coffee?
7. I'm going to order the same thing as Pierre
8. Can I pay later?
9. Can I change my reservation?
10. I'm going to Marseille now

Let's recap all the words we've learnt so far. How did you say these words in French?

1. something good
2. I've broken my...
3. I'm not
4. I don't feel
5. (to) eat
6. it wasn't
7. something
8. fine / well
9. I have reserved / I have booked
10. the same thing as her
11. expensive
12. if it's possible
13. my mum
14. some/any medicine
15. the same thing as Pierre
16. I ordered
17. (to) order
18. the same thing as me
19. Miss
20. how
21. some stamps / any stamps
22. I ate / I've eaten
23. something French
24. how are you?
25. a cold
26. I've caught
27. was
28. something + adjective
29. are you?
30. she isn't
31. in a hurry
32. are you going?
33. what
34. busy
35. for you
36. I'm not going
37. it was
38. the same thing as you
39. the flu
40. (to) see
41. a souvenir
42. (to) change it
43. today
44. a postcard
45. I'm doing well
46. another (a different type)
47. the same thing as him
48. (to) buy
49. in the name of
50. there is / there are
51. the same thing

52. is there? / are there?
53. Mrs
54. do you want?
55. (to) try it
56. I have
57. another (the same type) / again
58. (to) make/do it
59. I'm called
60. wasn't
61. he is
62. (to) change
63. I feel
64. (to) buy it
65. (to) drink
66. yesterday
67. I'm going
68. near here
69. is he?
70. I am
71. something from the region
72. now
73. she is
74. tired
75. is she?
76. I've hurt my...
77. ill
78. later
79. Mr
80. he isn't

1. quelque chose de bon
2. je me suis cassé...
3. je ne suis pas
4. je ne me sens pas
5. manger
6. ce n'était pas
7. quelque chose
8. bien
9. j'ai réservé
10. la même chose qu'elle
11. cher
12. si c'est possible
13. ma mère
14. un médicament
15. la même chose que Pierre
16. j'ai commandé
17. commander
18. la même chose que moi
19. mademoiselle (Mlle)
20. comment
21. des timbres
22. j'ai mangé
23. quelque chose de français
24. comment allez-vous?
25. un rhume
26. j'ai attrapé
27. était
28. quelque chose de + adjective
29. êtes-vous?
30. elle n'est pas
31. pressé
32. allez-vous?
33. que
34. occupé
35. pour vous
36. je ne vais pas
37. c'était
38. la même chose que vous
39. la grippe
40. voir
41. un souvenir
42. le changer
43. aujourd'hui
44. une carte postale
45. je vais bien
46. un/une autre
47. la même chose que lui
48. acheter
49. sous le nom de
50. il y a
51. la même chose
52. y a-t-il?
53. madame (Mme.)
54. voulez-vous?
55. l'essayer
56. j'ai
57. encore

58. le faire
59. je m'appelle
60. n'était pas
61. il est
62. changer
63. je me sens
64. l'acheter
65. boire
66. hier
67. je vais
68. près d'ici
69. est-il?

70. Je suis
71. quelque chose de la région
72. maintenant
73. elle est
74. fatigué
75. est-elle?
76. j'ai mal à...
77. malade
78. plus tard
79. monsieur (M.)
80. il n'est pas

LESSON 39

Let's start this lesson with a quick recap of the words and phrases we learnt in the last lesson. How do you say the following in French?

there is / there are
is there? / are there?
near here
(to) see

If there are any words you can't remember, go back to the last lesson and have a quick review of them before you start this lesson. It's really important that you remember the words you've learnt so far before you move on to learn any more.

Here is a good phrase to use to ask a question in French:

est-ce que c'est...?

It means "is it...?"
You pronounce it "es-skeugh-SEH"

Is it good?

"Est-ce que c'est..." means "is it...". Its literal meaning is "is it that it is..." (a bit weird, I know, but that's how they do it in French, so we won't judge).

Est-ce que c'est bon?
Is it good?
(literally: is it that it is good?)

Est-ce que c'est ici?
Is it here?
(literally: is it that it is here?)

Don't worry about what the literal meaning is though, I only told you just in case you wondered. Just learn "est-ce que c'est...?" as "is it...?".

How would you ask this in French?

Is it good?

Is it here?

Is it for me?

Is it good for me?

Is it good?
Est-ce que c'est bon?

Is it here?
Est-ce que c'est ici?

Is it for me?
Est-ce que c'est pour moi?

Is it good for me?
Est-ce que c'est bon pour moi?

How would you ask this in French?

Is that for me?

Is that everything?

Is it in France?

Is it near here?

Is that for me?
Est-ce que ça c'est pour moi?

Is that everything?
Est-ce que ça c'est tout?

Is it in France?
Est-ce que c'est en France?

Is it near here?
Est-ce que c'est près d'ici?

In the last lesson, we learnt the phrase "près d'ici",
which means "near here". Well, here's the opposite:

loin d'ici

It means "far from here"
You pronounce it "lwan(g) dee-SEE"

WORD LIST SO FAR

est-ce que c'est...? – *is it...?*
près d'ici – *near here*
loin d'ici – *far from here*

How would you say these sentences in French?

Is it far from here?

The restaurant isn't far from here.

I think it's too far from here.

That is too far from here.

Is it far from here?
Est-ce que c'est loin d'ici?

The restaurant isn't far from here.
Le restaurant n'est pas loin d'ici.

I think it's too far from here.
Pour moi, c'est trop loin d'ici.

That is too far from here.
Ça c'est trop loin d'ici.

If we take the "d'ici" bit away from "loin d'ici" we are left with this:

loin

It means "far"
You pronounce it "lwan(g)"

<u>WORD LIST SO FAR</u>

est-ce que c'est…? – *is it…?*
près d'ici – *near here*
loin d'ici – *far from here*
loin – *far*

How would you say these sentences in French?

Is it far?

It's very far.

I think it's too far.

It isn't far.

Is it far?
Est-ce que c'est loin?

It's very far.
C'est très loin.

I think it's too far.
Pour moi, c'est trop loin.

It isn't far.
Ce n'est pas loin.

Here's your next word in French, it's an adjective:

intéressant

It means "interesting"
You pronounce it "an-teh-reh-SON(g)"

WORD LIST SO FAR

est-ce que c'est...? – *is it...?*
près d'ici – *near here*
loin d'ici – *far from here*
loin – *far*
intéressant – *interesting*

How would you say these sentences in French?

Everything is very interesting here.

It isn't very interesting.

Everything is very interesting here.
Tout est très intéressant ici.

It isn't very interesting.
Ce n'est pas très intéressant.

How would you say this in French, keeping in mind that to make "intéressant" feminine, you simple add an 'e' to the end?

Marie is interesting.

Marie is interesting.
Marie est intéressante.

How would you say these sentences in French?

I think it's very interesting.

Everything is always very interesting here.

Everybody here is very interesting.

Is it interesting in Marseille?

I think it's very interesting.
Pour moi, c'est très intéressant.

Everything is always very interesting here.
Tout est toujours très intéressant ici.

Everybody here is very interesting.
Tout le monde ici est très intéressant.

Is it interesting in Marseille?
Est-ce que c'est intéressant à Marseille?

How would you say these sentences in French?

Is there anything interesting in La Rochelle? (*literally*: **something interesting**)

That is interesting.

Pierre is interesting.

Is there anything interesting in La Rochelle?
Y a-t-il quelque chose d'intéressant à La Rochelle?

That is interesting.
Ça c'est intéressant.

Pierre is interesting.
Pierre est intéressant.

Here's a useful word in French:

possible (de...)

It means "possible (to...)"
You pronounce it "poss-EEE-bleugh deugh"

Possible

Now, you can use "possible" just by itself:

ce n'est pas possible
it isn't possible

But, it becomes a really useful word If you put "de" after it.

Now, so far, we've learnt that "de" means "from" and "of" but here it means "to" ("Hang on!", I hear you scream, "I thought that 'à' meant 'to'". Well, yes it does as well...I know, make your mind up!) These little words (à and de) are called 'prepositions' and they can mean all sorts of things. We'll talk about them some more in a later lesson, but for now, just go with the flow.

But anyway, back to "possible de". You can put any verb after "possible de..." to mean "possible to...".

est-ce que c'est possible de payer demain?
is it possible to pay tomorrow?

est-ce que c'est possible de manger ici sans une réservation?
is it possible to eat here without a reservation?

So, how would you say these sentences in French?

Is it possible to try the wine?

Is it possible to see it now?

Is it possible to hire a car here?

It isn't possible to make a reservation.

It's possible to do it tomorrow.

Is it possible to try the wine?
Est-ce que c'est possible d'essayer le vin?

Is it possible to see it now?
Est-ce que c'est possible de le voir maintenant?

Is it possible to hire a car here?
Est-ce que c'est possible de louer une voiture ici?

It isn't possible to make a reservation.
Ce n'est pas possible de faire une réservation.

It's possible to do it tomorrow.
C'est possible de le faire demain.

Possible for me?

"Possible de..." means "possible to...". Therefore, "possible pour moi de..." must mean "possible for me to...".

Est-ce que c'est possible pour moi de payer demain?
Is it possible for me to pay tomorrow?

So, here's a quick clarification:

possible pour moi de...

It means "possible for me to..."
You pronounce it "poss-EEE-bleugh poor mwa deugh"

How would you say these sentences in French?

Is it possible for me to try the wine?

Is it possible for me to see it now?

Is it possible for me to hire a car for three days?

It isn't possible for me to do it now.

It wasn't possible for me to buy it; it was too expensive.

Is it possible for me to try the wine?
Est-ce que c'est possible pour moi d'essayer le vin?

Is it possible for me to see it now?
Est-ce que c'est possible pour moi de le voir maintenant?

Is it possible for me to hire a car for three days?
Est-ce que c'est possible pour moi de louer une voiture pour trois jours?

It isn't possible for me to do it now.
Ce n'est pas possible pour moi de le faire maintenant.

It wasn't possible for me to buy it; it was too expensive.
Ce n'était pas possible pour moi de l'acheter; c'était trop cher.

How would you say these sentences in French?

Everything is possible.

Is it possible for me to have two stamps, please?

Is it possible for me to change it?

Is it possible for me to go without you?

Is it possible for you to go without me?

Everything is possible.
Tout est possible.

Is it possible for me to have two stamps, please?
Est-ce que c'est possible pour moi d'avoir deux timbres, s'il vous plaît?

Is it possible for me to change it?
Est-ce que c'est possible pour moi de le changer?

Is it possible for me to go without you?
Est-ce que c'est possible pour moi d'aller sans vous?

Is it possible for you to go without me?
Est-ce que c'est possible pour vous d'aller sans moi?

WORD LIST SO FAR

est-ce que c'est...? – *is it...?*
près d'ici – *near here*
loin d'ici – *far from here*
loin– *far*
intéressant – *interesting*
possible (de...) – *possible (to...)*
possible pour moi de... – *possible for me to...*

It's time to practise what we've learnt in this lesson.

Grab a piece of paper and see if you can write down the following sentences in French. Then, you can check the answers.

1. Is it possible for me to eat here?
2. Is it possible for you to do that tomorrow?
3. Is it terrible?
4. I think it's very interesting
5. The theatre is far from here
6. The supermarket isn't near here
7. The post office isn't far from here
8. Is it beautiful?
9. It's too far from here
10. Is it expensive here?

1. Est-ce que c'est possible pour moi de manger ici?
2. Est-ce que c'est possible pour vous de faire ça demain?
3. Est-ce que c'est terrible?
4. Pour moi, c'est très intéressant
5. Le théâtre est loin d'ici
6. Le supermarché n'est pas près d'ici
7. La poste n'est pas loin d'ici
8. Est-ce que c'est beau?
9. C'est trop loin d'ici
10. Est-ce que c'est cher ici?

Now, let's have a go at doing some reverse translations. Again, write down the English translations of the following French sentences, then check to see if you were correct.

1. Est-ce que c'est bon?
2. Le parking n'est pas loin d'ici
3. L'arrêt de bus est près d'ici
4. Est-ce que c'est possible pour moi de commander maintenant?
5. Est-ce que c'est possible de payer par carte?
6. Marie est très intéressante
7. Est-ce que c'est possible pour moi de prendre un thé?
8. Ce n'est pas possible pour vous de louer une voiture
9. Est-ce que c'est pour moi?
10. Pierre n'est pas très intéressant

1. Is it good?
2. The car park isn't far from here
3. The bus stop is near here
4. Is it possible for me to order now?
5. Is it possible to pay by card?
6. Marie is very interesting
7. Is it possible for me to have a tea?
8. It isn't possible for you to hire a car
9. Is it for me?
10. Pierre isn't very interesting

What we're going to do now are some recap translations, which will incorporate words we learnt in the previous lesson.

1. I've caught the flu, have you got any medicine?
2. I've broken my finger
3. She isn't there
4. I'm too tired
5. Where are you going to have dinner?
6. Are you going to have some cheese?
7. No, I'm not Mr Boulot; I'm Mr Rouge
8. Do you want to pay by card?
9. Where can I buy some stamps?
10. Whom do I have to call?

1. J'ai attrapé la grippe, avez-vous du médicament?
2. Je me suis cassé le doigt
3. Elle n'est pas là
4. Je suis trop fatigué
5. Où allez-vous prendre le dîner?
6. Allez-vous prendre du fromage?
7. Non, je ne suis pas monsieur Boulot; je suis monsieur Rouge
8. Voulez-vous payer par carte?
9. Où puis-je acheter des timbres?
10. Qui dois-je appeler?

Let's now do some French to English recap translations. Grab a piece of paper and see if you can work out what these sentences mean.

1. Je voudrais acheter quelque chose de délicieux
2. J'ai une réservation sous le nom de Descartes
3. Je voudrais acheter un souvenir pour ma tante
4. J'ai mal à l'épaule
5. Il est très fatigué aujourd'hui
6. Marie est très occupée
7. Je suis pressé
8. Voulez-vous manger quelque chose?
9. Je vais essayer quelque chose de français
10. Je vais commander

1. I would like to buy something delicious
2. I have a reservation under the name of Descartes
3. I'd like to buy a souvenir for my auntie
4. I've hurt my shoulder
5. He's very tired today
6. Marie is very busy
7. I'm in a hurry
8. Do you want to eat something?
9. I'm going to try something French
10. I'm going to order

Let's recap all the words we've learnt so far. How did you say these words in French?

1. do you want?
2. it wasn't
3. far from here
4. a postcard
5. if it's possible
6. I've hurt my...
7. is there? / are there?
8. now
9. (to) eat
10. I am
11. tired
12. something French
13. ill
14. I'm called
15. (to) make/do it
16. Mrs
17. she is
18. interesting
19. the same thing as Pierre
20. something
21. possible (to...)
22. near here
23. was
24. the same thing as him
25. the flu
26. another (the same type) / again
27. busy
28. (to) buy
29. (to) change it
30. I ordered
31. the same thing as her
32. the same thing
33. I'm not going
34. Miss
35. later
36. I've caught
37. wasn't
38. (to) change
39. a cold
40. are you?
41. I have reserved / I have booked
42. in the name of
43. what
44. possible for me to...
45. Mr
46. something from the region
47. he isn't
48. I'm going
49. for you
50. the same thing as you
51. some stamps / any stamps

52. I'm doing well
53. something + adjective
54. (to) see
55. some/any medicine
56. a souvenir
57. how are you?
58. fine / well
59. (to) drink
60. is he?
61. I don't feel
62. I ate / I've eaten
63. far
64. I'm not
65. she isn't
66. I have
67. he is
68. how
69. yesterday
70. I've broken my...
71. is she?
72. expensive
73. my mum
74. (to) try it
75. today
76. in a hurry
77. is it...?
78. (to) buy it
79. it was
80. another (a different type)
81. there is / there are
82. are you going?
83. (to) order
84. I feel
85. the same thing as me
86. something good

1. voulez-vous?
2. ce n'était pas
3. loin d'ici
4. une carte postale
5. si c'est possible
6. j'ai mal à...
7. y a-t-il?
8. maintenant
9. manger
10. Je suis
11. fatigué
12. quelque chose de français
13. malade
14. je m'appelle
15. le faire
16. madame (Mme.)
17. elle est
18. intéressant
19. la même chose que Pierre
20. quelque chose
21. possible (de...)
22. près d'ici
23. était
24. la même chose que lui
25. la grippe
26. encore
27. occupé
28. acheter
29. le changer
30. j'ai commandé
31. la même chose qu'elle
32. la même chose
33. je ne vais pas
34. mademoiselle (Mlle)
35. plus tard
36. j'ai attrapé
37. n'était pas
38. changer
39. un rhume
40. êtes-vous?
41. j'ai réservé
42. sous le nom de
43. que
44. possible pour moi de...
45. monsieur (M.)
46. quelque chose de la région
47. il n'est pas
48. je vais
49. pour vous
50. la même chose que vous
51. des timbres
52. je vais bien
53. quelque chose de + adjective
54. voir
55. un médicament
56. un souvenir
57. comment allez-vous?

58. bien
59. boire
60. est-il?
61. je ne me sens pas
62. j'ai mangé
63. loin
64. je ne suis pas
65. elle n'est pas
66. j'ai
67. il est
68. comment
69. hier
70. je me suis cassé...
71. est-elle?
72. cher
73. ma mère

74. l'essayer
75. aujourd'hui
76. pressé
77. est-ce que c'est...?
78. l'acheter
79. c'était
80. un/une autre
81. il y a
82. allez-vous?
83. commander
84. je me sens
85. la même chose que moi
86. quelque chose de bon

LESSON 40

Let's start this lesson with a quick recap of the words and phrases we learnt in the last lesson. How do you say the following in French?

is it...?
near here
far from here
interesting
possible (to...)
possible for me to...

If there are any words you can't remember, go back to the last lesson and have a quick review of them before you start this lesson. It's really important that you remember the words you've learnt so far before you move on to learn any more.

Now, we've already had "changer", which means "to change". Well, let's add that little word "de" to the end of it:

changer de

It also means "(to) change"
You pronounce it "shon-JSHAY deugh"

To change

Now, we've had two ways (albeit extremely similar) to say "change": "changer" and "changer de".

There is a slight difference between the two.

CHANGER – to change (to modify something)
   Je voudrais changer ma réservation
   I would like to change (modify) my reservation

CHANGER DE – to change (to exchange or switch)
   Je voudrais changer de table
   I would like to change (switch) tables

How would you say these sentences in French?

I would like to change tables.

Can I change hotels?

I would like to change tables.
Je voudrais changer de table.

Can I change hotels?
Puis-je changer d'hôtel?

One thing you might notice is that in English, when you want to change something, you tend to say the thing in the plural "change tables" or "change hotels". In French, however, you leave it in the singular "changer de table" or "changer d'hôtel".

Change cars

To help understand the difference between "changer" and "changer de", let me show you an example I used to use to get my head around it.

Je voudrais changer de voiture
I would like to change cars
(get a whole new car)

Je voudrais changer la voiture
I would like to change the car
(modify it somehow – maybe paint it or decorate it)

WORD LIST SO FAR

changer – *(to) change (to modify)*
changer de – *(to) change (to exchange)*

How would you say these sentences in French?

I'm going to change cars.

Do I have to change tables?

Can I change rooms?

Are you going to change hotels?

I'm going to change cars.
Je vais changer de voiture.

Do I have to change tables?
Dois-je changer de table?

Can I change rooms?
Puis-je changer de chambre?

Are you going to change hotels?
Allez-vous changer d'hôtel?

This next word is always a useful one to have if something goes wrong:

un problème

It means "a problem"
You pronounce it "an(g) prob-LEMM"

WORD LIST SO FAR

changer – *(to) change (to modify)*
changer de – *(to) change (to exchange)*
un problème – *a problem*

So, how would you say these sentences in French?

I have a problem.

There's a problem with Pierre.

There is a problem with my car.

Is there a problem, Mr Blanc?

There's a big problem in Paris today.

What is the problem?

I have a problem.
J'ai un problème.

There's a problem with Pierre.
Il y a un problème avec Pierre.

There is a problem with my car.
Il y a un problème avec ma voiture.

Is there a problem, Mr Blanc?
Y a-t-il un problème, Monsieur Blanc?

There's a big problem in Paris today.
Il y a un grand problème à Paris aujourd'hui.

What is the problem?
Quel est le problème?

This is also a nice little phrase to have and memorise:

pas de problème

It means "no problem" or literally, "not any problem"
You pronounce it "pad prob-LEMM"

WORD LIST SO FAR

changer – *(to) change (to modify)*
changer de – *(to) change (to exchange)*
un problème – *a problem*
pas de problème – *no problem*

How would you say this in French?

No, no problem.

No, no problem.

Non, pas de problème.

The "pas de" bit in "pas de problème" means "not any", so you might be able to guess what this phrase means:

il n'y a pas de...

It means "there isn't any" or "there aren't any"
You pronounce it "eel-nee-ah-pad"

WORD LIST SO FAR

changer – *(to) change (to modify)*
changer de – *(to) change (to exchange)*
un problème – *a problem*
pas de problème – *no problem*
il n'y a pas de… – *there isn't any… / there aren't any…*

So, how would you say these sentences in French?

There isn't any wine.

There isn't a television.

There is no problem.

Can I change rooms; there's no shower?

Excuse me, there's no water.

There isn't any wine.
Il n'y a pas de vin.

There isn't a television.
Il n'y a pas de télévision.

There is no problem.
Il n'y a pas de problème.

Can I change rooms; there's no shower?
Puis-je changer de chambre; il n'y a pas de douche?

Excuse me, there's no water.
Excusez-moi, il n'y a pas d'eau.

Here is your last phrase for this lesson:

dans la chambre

It means "in the room"
You pronounce it "don(g) lah SHOM-breugh"

WORD LIST SO FAR

changer – *(to) change (to modify)*
changer de – *(to) change (to exchange)*
un problème – *a problem*
pas de problème – *no problem*
il n'y a pas de... – *there isn't any... / there aren't any...*
dans la chambre – *in the room*

How would you say these sentences in French?

Is there a television in the room?

Can I eat in the room?

Are you in the room?

Excuse me, there's no bed in the room.

It's in the room.

It wasn't in the room.

Is there a television in the room?
Y a-t-il une télévision dans la chambre?

Can I eat in the room?
Puis-je manger dans la chambre?

Are you in the room?
Êtes-vous dans la chambre?

Excuse me, there's no bed in the room.
Excusez-moi, il n'y a pas de lit dans la chambre.

It's in the room.
C'est dans la chambre.

It wasn't in the room.
Ce n'était pas dans la chambre.

WORD LIST SO FAR

changer – *(to) change (to modify)*
changer de – *(to) change (to exchange)*
un problème – *a problem*
pas de problème – *no problem*
il n'y a pas de... – *there isn't any... / there aren't any...*
dans la chambre – *in the room*

It's time to practise what we've learnt in this lesson.

Grab a piece of paper and see if you can write down the following sentences in French. Then, you can check the answers.

1. Are you going to change tables?
2. Is it possible for me to change rooms?
3. There isn't a problem
4. It was in the room
5. Excuse me, there's no bed in the room
6. Is it in the room?
7. I would like to change hotels
8. Do you have a problem?
9. There's a problem; the light doesn't work
10. Is there a problem?

1. Allez-vous changer de table?
2. Est-ce que c'est possible pour moi de changer de chambre?
3. Il n'y a pas de problème
4. C'était dans la chambre
5. Excusez-moi, il n'y a pas de lit dans la chambre
6. Est-ce que c'est dans la chambre?
7. Je voudrais changer d'hôtel
8. Avez-vous un problème?
9. Il y a un problème; la lumière ne marche pas
10. Y a-t-il un problème?

Now, let's have a go at doing some reverse translations. Again, write down the English translations of the following French sentences, then check to see if you were correct.

1. Dois-je changer de table?
2. Quand allez-vous changer de voiture?
3. Y a-t-il un problème avec la voiture?
4. Je voudrais changer de chambre
5. Il n'y a pas d'eau
6. Il y a un problème avec la télévision dans ma chambre
7. Il n'y a pas d'électricité
8. Êtes-vous dans la chambre?
9. Puis-je changer de chambre; il n'y a pas de douche
10. La douche dans ma chambre ne marche pas

1. Do I have to change tables?
2. When are you going to change cars?
3. Is there a problem with the car?
4. I would like to change rooms
5. There's no water
6. There's a problem with the television in my room
7. There's no electricity
8. Are you in the room?
9. Can I change rooms; there's no shower
10. The shower in my room doesn't work

What we're going to do now are some recap translations, which will incorporate words we learnt in the previous lessons.

1. Can I buy a postcard here?
2. Are you going to have dinner at the hotel?
3. She isn't tired
4. Can I pay the bill later?
5. I'm going to the toilet
6. I'm doing well
7. I have something for my sister
8. Are you going to hire a car?
9. The hotel is near me
10. Everybody was very nice here

1. Puis-je acheter une carte postale ici?
2. Allez-vous prendre le dîner à l'hôtel?
3. Elle n'est pas fatiguée
4. Puis-je payer l'addition plus tard?
5. Je vais aux toilettes
6. Je vais bien
7. J'ai quelque chose pour ma sœur
8. Allez-vous louer une voiture?
9. L'hôtel est près de moi
10. Tout le monde était très sympa ici

Let's now do some French to English recap translations. Grab a piece of paper and see if you can work out what these sentences mean.

1. Je voudrais l'acheter pour ma femme
2. Où puis-je manger?
3. Puis-je l'apporter à Paris?
4. La gare n'est pas près d'ici
5. Je ne vais pas manger à l'hôtel
6. Y a-t-il un bon restaurant près d'ici?
7. Comment allez-vous payer?
8. Qu'allez-vous faire ce soir?
9. Je me suis cassé le bras
10. Allez-vous commander maintenant?

1. I'd like to buy it for my wife
2. Where can I eat?
3. Can I bring it to Paris?
4. The train station isn't near here
5. I'm not going to eat at the hotel
6. Is there a good restaurant near here?
7. How are you going to pay?
8. What are you going to do this evening?
9. I've broken my arm
10. Are you going to order now?

Let's recap all the words we've learnt so far. How did you say these words in French?

1. now
2. (to) change it
3. far
4. I ordered
5. in a hurry
6. (to) eat
7. it was
8. ill
9. (to) drink
10. something good
11. some/any medicine
12. I've hurt my...
13. no problem
14. something French
15. I have reserved / I have booked
16. something
17. possible for me to...
18. if it's possible
19. I ate / I've eaten
20. the same thing as you
21. something from the region
22. I've broken my...
23. a postcard
24. a problem
25. it wasn't
26. the same thing as me
27. the same thing as him
28. the flu
29. I'm going
30. the same thing as Pierre
31. today
32. another (the same type) / again
33. are you going?
34. in the name of
35. I have
36. there is / there are
37. Mr
38. (to) see
39. I've caught
40. later
41. (to) change (modify)
42. Miss
43. he is
44. some stamps / any stamps
45. (to) order
46. (to) try it
47. (to) buy
48. in the room
49. Mrs
50. I am
51. are you?
52. my mum

53. a cold
54. interesting
55. far from here
56. is she?
57. for you
58. is it...?
59. fine / well
60. do you want?
61. I'm not going
62. I don't feel
63. is he?
64. (to) change (exchange)
65. there isn't any... / there aren't any...
66. is there? / are there?
67. expensive
68. what
69. I'm doing well
70. (to) buy it
71. a souvenir
72. how
73. I'm called
74. was
75. I feel
76. possible (to...)
77. something + adjective
78. tired
79. wasn't
80. (to) make/do it
81. another (a different type)
82. she is
83. I'm not
84. how are you?
85. she isn't
86. near here
87. busy
88. the same thing
89. the same thing as her
90. he isn't
91. yesterday

1. maintenant
2. le changer
3. loin
4. j'ai commandé
5. pressé
6. manger
7. c'était
8. malade
9. boire
10. quelque chose de bon
11. un médicament
12. j'ai mal à...
13. pas de problème
14. quelque chose de français
15. j'ai réservé
16. quelque chose
17. possible pour moi de...
18. si c'est possible
19. j'ai mangé
20. la même chose que vous
21. quelque chose de la région
22. je me suis cassé...
23. une carte postale
24. un problème
25. ce n'était pas
26. la même chose que moi
27. la même chose que lui
28. la grippe
29. je vais
30. la même chose que Pierre
31. aujourd'hui
32. encore
33. allez-vous?
34. sous le nom de
35. j'ai
36. il y a
37. monsieur (M.)
38. voir
39. j'ai attrapé
40. plus tard
41. changer
42. mademoiselle (Mlle)
43. il est
44. des timbres
45. commander
46. l'essayer
47. acheter
48. dans la chambre
49. madame (Mme.)
50. je suis
51. êtes-vous?
52. ma mère
53. un rhume
54. intéressant
55. loin d'ici
56. est-elle?
57. pour vous

58. est-ce que c'est...?
59. bien
60. voulez-vous?
61. je ne vais pas
62. je ne me sens pas
63. est-il?
64. changer de
65. il n'y a pas de...
66. y a-t-il?
67. cher
68. que
69. je vais bien
70. l'acheter
71. un souvenir
72. comment
73. je m'appelle
74. était
75. je me sens
76. possible (de...)

77. quelque chose de + adjective
78. fatigué
79. n'était pas
80. le faire
81. un/une autre
82. elle est
83. je ne suis pas
84. comment allez-vous?
85. elle n'est pas
86. près d'ici
87. occupé
88. la même chose
89. la même chose qu'elle
90. il n'est pas
91. hier

LESSON 41

Let's start this lesson with a quick recap of the words and phrases we learnt in the last lesson. How do you say the following in French?

(to) change (to modify)
(to) change (to exchange)
a problem
no problem
there isn't any / there aren't any
in the room

If there are any words you can't remember, go back to the last lesson and have a quick review of them before you start this lesson. It's really important that you remember the words you've learnt so far before you move on to learn any more.

Now, we've had "trop" before, but let's add a little more:

trop de bruit

It means "too much noise"
You pronounce it "troh deugh brwee"

WORD LIST SO FAR

trop de bruit – *too much noise*

How would you say these sentences in French?

There is too much noise.

There is always too much noise here.

It's good but there's too much noise.

Do you want to go to the hotel; there is too much noise here?

Is there too much noise for you?

There's too much noise in my room.

There is too much noise.
Il y a trop de bruit.

There is always too much noise here.
Il y a toujours trop de bruit ici.

It's good but there's too much noise.
C'est bon mais il y a trop de bruit.

Do you want to go to the hotel; there is too much noise here?
Voulez-vous aller à l'hôtel; il y a trop de bruit ici?

Is there too much noise for you?
Y a-t-il trop de bruit pour vous?

There's too much noise in my room.
Il y a trop de bruit dans ma chambre.

This phrase is similar to "trop de bruit":

trop de cafards

It means "too many cockroaches"
You pronounce it "troh deugh kah-FAHR"

WORD LIST SO FAR

trop de bruit – *too much noise*
trop de cafards – *too many cockroaches*

How would you say these sentences in French?

There are too many cockroaches in the room.

There are too many cockroaches here.

It's beautiful here but I think there are too many cockroaches.

There are too many cockroaches in the room.
Il y a trop de cafards dans la chambre.

There are too many cockroaches here.
Il y a trop de cafards ici.

It's beautiful here but I think there are too many cockroaches.
C'est beau ici mais pour moi, il y a trop de cafards.

Too much

You've probably noticed that we've used "trop de…" to mean "too much" and also "too many". You can put any noun on the end of "trop de" and if the noun is singular, it means "too much" in English, but if the noun is plural, it means "too many" in English.

trop de vin
too much wine

trop de poulet
too much chicken

trop de carottes
too many carrots

If you just want to say "too much" or "too many" by itself, you just say "trop" without the "de".

c'est trop pour moi
it's too much for me

Remember how "tout le monde" means "everybody". Well...:

trop de monde

It means "too many people"
You pronounce it "troh deugh mond"

How would you say this in French?

There are too many people here.

There are too many people here.
Il y a trop de monde ici.

Too many people

There are actually a couple of ways to say "too many people" in French. The first phrase, "trop de monde" is just one way. The word "monde" means "world" in French, so "trop de monde" really means "too much of the world".

The second way is just to use the word for "people" that we've already learnt, "personnes".

trop de monde
too many people

trop de personnes
too many people

WORD LIST SO FAR

trop de bruit – *too much noise*
trop de cafards – *too many cockroaches*
trop de... – *too much... / too many...*
trop de monde – *too many people*
trop de personnes – *too many people*

How would you say these sentences in French?

Paris is very beautiful but there are always too many people there.

I think there are too many people there.

There are always too many people at this restaurant.

Paris is very beautiful but there are always too many people there.

Paris est très beau mais il y a toujours trop de monde/personnes là.

I think there are too many people there.

Pour moi, il y a trop de monde/personnes là.

There are always too many people at this restaurant.

Il y a toujours trop de monde/personnes à ce restaurant.

Here's another useful phrase to add to your collection:

beaucoup (de)

It means "a lot (of)"
You pronounce it "boe-koo deugh"

WORD LIST SO FAR

trop de bruit – *too much noise*
trop de cafards – *too many cockroaches*
trop de... – *too much... / too many...*
trop de monde – *too many people*
trop de personnes – *too many people*
beaucoup de – *a lot of*

How would you say these sentences in French?

There is a lot of noise.

There are lots of people here.

There is a lot of wine here.

Why do you have lots of cars?

There is a lot of noise.
Il y a beaucoup de bruit.

There are lots of people here.
Il y a beaucoup de personnes ici.
(or : il y a beaucoup de monde ici)

There is a lot of wine here.
Il y a beaucoup de vin ici.

Why do you have lots of cars?
Pourquoi avez-vous beaucoup de voitures?

How would you say these sentences in French?

I would like to eat here but there are lots of cockroaches in the restaurant.

There isn't a lot of cheese.

There is always a lot of food here.

I would like to eat here but there are lots of cockroaches in the restaurant.
Je voudrais manger ici mais il y a beaucoup de cafards dans le restaurant.

There isn't a lot of cheese.
Il n'y a pas beaucoup de fromage.

There is always a lot of food here.
Il y a toujours beaucoup de nourriture ici.

Here's your last word for this lesson:

choses (à...)

It means "things (to...)"
You pronounce it "shoze ah"

Things to do

Remember how a couple of lessons ago, we had "possible de...", meaning "possible to...".. Whenever you use "possible" with a verb, you have to put "de" in between them.

ce n'est pas possible de partir
it isn't possible to leave

The same thing happens with "choses". If you want to put a verb after "choses", you have to use "à".

il y a beaucoup de choses à faire
there are lots of things to do

How would you say these sentences in French?

I have too many things to do.

There are lots of things to eat.

There are lots of things to see in France.

There are always lots of things to do in Marseille but there are also lots of people.

I have too many things to do.
J'ai trop de choses à faire.

There are lots of things to eat.
Il y a beaucoup de choses à manger.

There are lots of things to see in France.
Il y a beaucoup de choses à voir en France.

There are always lots of things to do in Marseille but there are also lots of people.
Il y a toujours beaucoup de choses à faire à Marseille mais il y a aussi beaucoup de personnes.

How would you say these sentences in French?

I bought lots of things to eat yesterday.

Do you have lots of things to do?

There aren't a lot of things to eat.

I bought lots of things to eat yesterday.

J'ai acheté beaucoup de choses à manger hier.

Do you have lots of things to do?

Avez-vous beaucoup de choses à faire?

There aren't a lot of things to eat.

Il n'y a pas beaucoup de choses à manger.

WORD LIST SO FAR

trop de bruit – *too much noise*
trop de cafards – *too many cockroaches*
trop de... – *too much... / too many...*
trop de monde – *too many people*
trop de personnes – *too many people*
beaucoup de – *a lot of*
choses à... – *things to...*

It's time to practise what we've learnt in this lesson.

Grab a piece of paper and see if you can write down the following sentences in French. Then, you can check the answers.

1. Can I change rooms; there's too much noise in my room?
2. I like it here but there are too many cockroaches
3. It's beautiful but there are always too many people here
4. There's a lot of food here
5. I think there are lots of things to do
6. There isn't a lot of wine here for everybody
7. Do you have things to eat at the hotel?
8. There is too much noise at the hotel
9. There are too many people and I don't have a lot of food
10. I have a headache; there is too much noise

1. Puis-je changer de chambre; il y a trop de bruit dans ma chambre?
2. Je l'aime ici mais il y a trop de cafards
3. C'est beau mais il y a toujours trop de personnes/monde ici
4. Il y a beaucoup de nourriture ici
5. Pour moi, il y a beaucoup de choses à faire
6. Il n'y a pas beaucoup de vin ici pour tout le monde
7. Avez-vous choses à manger à l'hôtel?
8. Il y a trop de bruit à l'hôtel
9. Il y a trop de personnes/monde et je n'ai pas beaucoup de nourriture
10. J'ai mal à la tête; il y a trop de bruit

Now, let's have a go at doing some reverse translations.

1. J'aime la France; il y a beaucoup de vin et beaucoup de fromage. C'est parait pour moi
2. Il y a beaucoup de personnes/monde ici mais tout le monde est très sympa
3. Il y a beaucoup de cafards dans ma chambre
4. Pour moi, il y a trop de voitures à Paris
5. Il y a beaucoup de choses à faire et à voir à Marseille; c'est absolument beau
6. Il y a beaucoup de choses à manger mais j'ai mal à l'estomac
7. Il y a toujours beaucoup de nourriture chez Marie
8. Pour moi, il n'y a pas beaucoup de choses à faire mais c'est très beau
9. J'ai trop de carottes mais tout est délicieux
10. C'est bon mais il y a trop de bruit

1. I like France; there's a lot of wine and a lot of cheese. It's perfect for me
2. There are a lot of people here but everybody is very nice
3. There are lots of cockroaches in my room
4. I think there are too many cars in Paris
5. There are lots of things to do and see in Marseille; it's absolutely beautiful
6. There are lots of things to eat but I have a stomach ache
7. There is always a lot of food at Marie's house
8. I think there aren't a lot of things to do but it's very beautiful
9. I have too many carrots but everything is delicious
10. It's good but there is too much noise

What we're going to do now are some recap translations, which will incorporate words we learnt in the previous lessons.

1. I would like a bottle of wine for the table, please
2. This restaurant is perfect
3. I think the food here is always very good
4. The dinner yesterday was fantastic but the wine wasn't very good
5. Excuse me, what time is it?
6. The cars here are one hundred euros per week
7. The reservation is at 8pm
8. It isn't near but the bus isn't very expensive
9. Is it good for me?
10. Is it possible for me to take the train?

1. Je voudrais une bouteille de vin pour la table, s'il vous plaît
2. Ce restaurant est parfait
3. Pour moi, la nourriture ici est toujours très bonne
4. Le dîner hier était fantastique mais le vin n'était pas très bon
5. Excusez-moi, quelle heure est-il?
6. Les voitures ici sont cent euros par semaine
7. La réservation est à huit heures le soir
8. Ce n'est pas près mais le bus n'est pas très cher
9. Est-ce que c'est bon pour moi?
10. Est-ce que c'est possible pour moi de prendre le train?

Let's now do some French to English recap translations. Grab a piece of paper and see if you can work out what these sentences mean.

1. Je voudrais trois timbres, s'il vous plaît
2. Excusez-moi, c'est combien ça?
3. Puis-je changer la réservation?
4. Avez-vous une plus grande voiture?
5. Que voulez-vous acheter?
6. Voulez-vous l'essayer?
7. Je voudrais acheter quelque chose ici mais les souvenirs sont trop chers
8. Où puis-je acheter une carte postale de la région?
9. Ma mère est ici mais mon père est à Paris
10. Allez-vous voir la Tour Eiffel?

1. I would like three stamps, please
2. Excuse me, how much is that?
3. Can I change the reservation?
4. Do you have a bigger car?
5. What do you want to buy?
6. Do you want to try it?
7. I would like to buy something but the souvenirs are too expensive
8. Where can I buy a postcard from the region?
9. My mum is here but my dad is in Paris
10. Are you going to see the Eiffel Tower?

Let's recap all the words we've learnt so far. How did you say these words in French?

1. Miss
2. something from the region
3. I'm going
4. it wasn't
5. I've caught
6. something French
7. there is / there are
8. possible (to...)
9. things to...
10. is he?
11. too much... / too many...
12. possible for me to...
13. (to) change it
14. the same thing as you
15. if it's possible
16. (to) see
17. later
18. in the room
19. (to) change (modify)
20. no problem
21. I'm called
22. how
23. I'm doing well
24. are you?
25. something
26. something + adjective
27. expensive
28. something good
29. a cold
30. some stamps / any stamps
31. busy
32. the same thing as him
33. are you going?
34. too many people
35. how are you?
36. I have
37. I don't feel
38. near here
39. (to) change (exchange)
40. she isn't
41. is it...?
42. (to) drink
43. do you want?
44. the flu
45. I have reserved / I have booked
46. too much noise
47. what
48. the same thing as me
49. there isn't any... / there aren't any...

50. another (the same type) / again
51. I've hurt my...
52. a problem
53. far
54. he isn't
55. (to) order
56. interesting
57. I'm not
58. was
59. I am
60. today
61. a souvenir
62. tired
63. my mum
64. fine / well
65. I ordered
66. (to) buy
67. Mrs
68. is there? / are there?
69. I'm not going
70. (to) try it
71. the same thing as Pierre
72. yesterday
73. for you
74. (to) make/do it
75. in the name of
76. is she?
77. ill
78. he is
79. far from here
80. it was
81. (to) buy it
82. a postcard
83. I've broken my...
84. now
85. the same thing
86. she is
87. I ate / I've eaten
88. too many cockroaches
89. in a hurry
90. (to) eat
91. the same thing as her
92. I feel
93. a lot of
94. some/any medicine
95. another (a different type)
96. Mr
97. wasn't

2. mademoiselle (Mlle)
3. quelque chose de la région
4. je vais
5. ce n'était pas
6. j'ai attrapé
7. quelque chose de français
8. il y a
9. possible (de...)
10. choses à...
11. est-il?
12. trop de...
13. possible pour moi de...
14. le changer
15. la même chose que vous
16. si c'est possible
17. voir
18. plus tard
19. dans la chambre
20. changer
21. pas de problème
22. je m'appelle
23. comment
24. je vais bien
25. êtes-vous?
26. quelque chose
27. quelque chose de + adjective
28. cher
29. quelque chose de bon
30. un rhume
31. des timbres
32. occupé
33. la même chose que lui
34. allez-vous?
35. trop de monde / trop de personnes
36. comment allez-vous?
37. j'ai
38. je ne me sens pas
39. près d'ici
40. changer de
41. elle n'est pas
42. est-ce que c'est...?
43. boire
44. voulez-vous?
45. la grippe
46. j'ai réservé
47. trop de bruit
48. que
49. la même chose que moi
50. il n'y a pas de...

51. encore
52. j'ai mal à...
53. un problème
54. loin
55. il n'est pas
56. commander
57. intéressant
58. je ne suis pas
59. était
60. je suis
61. aujourd'hui
62. un souvenir
63. fatigué
64. ma mère
65. bien
66. j'ai commandé
67. acheter
68. madame (Mme.)
69. y a-t-il?
70. je ne vais pas
71. l'essayer
72. la même chose que Pierre
73. hier
74. pour vous
75. le faire

76. sous le nom de
77. est-elle?
78. malade
79. il est
80. loin d'ici
81. c'était
82. l'acheter
83. une carte postale
84. je me suis cassé...
85. maintenant
86. la même chose
87. elle est
88. j'ai mangé
89. trop de cafards
90. pressé
91. manger
92. la même chose qu'elle
93. je me sens
94. beaucoup de
95. un médicament
96. un/une autre
97. monsieur (M.)
98. n'était pas

LESSON 42

Let's start this lesson with a quick recap of the words and phrases we learnt in the last lesson. How do you say the following in French?

too much noise
too many cockroaches
too many people
a lot of / lots of
things (to...)

If there are any words you can't remember, go back to the last lesson and have a quick review of them before you start this lesson. It's really important that you remember the words you've learnt so far before you move on to learn any more.

Here's a very useful joining word in French:

parce que

It means "because"
You pronounce it "parsk"

WORD LIST SO FAR

parce que – *because*

How would you ask this in French?

I'm not going to eat here because the food is terrible.

I'm not going to the beach because I'm too tired.

I'm very busy because I have lots of things to do.

I'm not going to buy that because it's too expensive.

I'm not going to eat here because the food is terrible.

Je ne vais pas manger ici parce que la nourriture est terrible.

I'm not going to the beach because I'm too tired.

Je ne vais pas à la plage parce que je suis trop fatigué.

I'm very busy because I have lots of things to do.

Je suis très occupé parce que j'ai beaucoup de choses à faire.

I'm not going to buy that because it's too expensive.

Je ne vais pas acheter ça parce que c'est trop cher.

How would you ask this in French?

Can you pay because my card doesn't work?

I don't like that because it's green.

I like it because it's beautiful.

Can you pay because my card doesn't work?

Pouvez-vous payer parce que ma carte ne marche pas?

I don't like that because it's green.

Je n'aime pas ça parce que c'est vert.

I like it because it's beautiful.

Je l'aime parce que c'est beau.

We've had "j'ai", which means "I have", well, here's the opposite:

je n'ai pas

It means "I don't have" or "I haven't"
You pronounce it "jsheugh nay pah"

WORD LIST SO FAR

parce que – *because*
je n'ai pas – *I haven't / I don't have*

What you can do is replace any phrase that has "j'ai" in it with "je n'ai pas". So, how would you say these sentences in French?

I haven't ordered.

I haven't eaten today.

I don't have many things to do today.

I don't have a reservation but I would like a table for two.

I haven't ordered.
Je n'ai pas commandé.

I haven't eaten today.
Je n'ai pas mangé aujourd'hui.

I don't have many things to do today.
Je n'ai pas beaucoup de choses à faire aujourd'hui.

I don't have a reservation but I would like a table for two.
Je n'ai pas une réservation mais je voudrais une table pour deux.

How would you say these sentences in French?

I haven't tried the pizza.

I haven't paid the bill.

I haven't eaten a lot today.

I haven't ordered the wine.

I haven't tried the pizza.
Je n'ai pas essayé la pizza.

I haven't paid the bill.
Je n'ai pas payé l'addition.

I haven't eaten a lot today.
Je n'ai pas mangé beaucoup aujourd'hui.

I haven't ordered the wine.
Je n'ai pas commandé le vin.

Here's your next phrase in French:

le temps (de...)

It means "the time (to...)"
You pronounce it "leugh ton(g) deugh"

The time

We've already had the word "l'heure", which means the time on a watch.

je n'ai pas l'heure
I don't have the time (on a watch)
I don't know what time it is

Avez-vous l'heure?
Do you have the time (on a watch)?
Do you know what time it is?

The word "le temps" is actually talking about the time to do something, not the time on a clock.

je n'ai pas le temps
I don't have the time
I'm not free / I'm too busy

If you want to put a verb on the end of "le temps" you have to use the little word "de" first.

je n'ai pas le temps de faire une réservation
I don't have the time to make a reservation

How would you say these sentences in French?

I would like to do it but I don't have the time.

I don't have the time to do it now.

Do you have time tomorrow?

Do you have time to go to the beach today?

Do you have the time to do it for me now?

I would like to do it but I don't have the time.

Je voudrais le faire mais je n'ai pas le temps.

I don't have the time to do it now.

Je n'ai pas le temps de le faire maintenant.

Do you have time tomorrow?

Avez-vous le temps demain?

Do you have time to go to the beach today?

Avez-vous le temps d'aller à la plage aujourd'hui?

Do you have the time to do it for me now?

Avez-vous le temps de le faire pour moi maintenant?

Here's a useful phrase in French:

je n'ai pas de...

It means "I don't have any..."
You pronounce it "jsheugh nay pah deugh"

Not any

The words "pas de" in French, literally mean "not any". So, a couple of lessons ago, when we learnt "no problem" – "pas de problème", what it literally means is "not any problem".

You can use "pas de..." with any noun to mean "not any..." or "not a...".

je n'ai pas de temps
I don't have any time

je n'ai pas d'argent
I don't have any money

je n'ai pas d'amis
I don't have any friends 🙁

So, how would you say this in French?

I don't have any cake for you.

I don't have any cake for you.
Je n'ai pas de gâteau pour vous.

Here's another useful phrase in French:

avec moi

It means "with me"
You pronounce it "ah-VEK mwah"

WORD LIST SO FAR

parce que – *because*
je n'ai pas – *I haven't / I don't have*
je n'ai pas de – *I don't have any*
le temps (de...) – *the time (to...)*
avec moi – *with me*

How would you say these sentences in French?

I don't have any money with me.

I don't have the tickets with me.

Do you want to go to the beach with me tomorrow?

Can you pay the bill because I don't have my card with me?

I don't have any money with me.
Je n'ai pas d'argent avec moi.

I don't have the tickets with me.
Je n'ai pas les billets avec moi.

Do you want to go to the beach
with me tomorrow?
**Voulez-vous aller à la plage avec
moi demain?**

Can you pay the bill because I
don't have my card with me?
**Pouvez-vous payer l'addition
parce que je n'ai pas ma carte
avec moi?**

You might be able to guess what this phrase means:

je n'ai pas réservé

It means "I haven't reserved" or "I haven't booked"
You pronounce it "jsheugh nay pas reh-zair-vay"

WORD LIST SO FAR

parce que – *because*
je n'ai pas – *I haven't / I don't have*
je n'ai pas de – *I don't have any*
le temps (de...) – *the time (to...)*
avec moi – *with me*
je n'ai pas réservé – *I haven't reserved/booked*

How would you say these sentences in French?

I haven't booked a table but I would like to eat here, if it's possible.

I haven't booked a table because it isn't very busy at the restaurant.

I haven't booked a table but I would like to eat here, if it's possible.

Je n'ai pas réservé une table mais je voudrais manger ici, si c'est possible.

I haven't booked a table because it isn't very busy at the restaurant.

Je n'ai pas réservé une table parce que ce n'est pas très occupé au restaurant.

Here's a verb for you to add to your verb collection:

apporter

It means "(to) bring"
You pronounce it "ah-poor-TAY"

WORD LIST SO FAR

parce que – *because*
je n'ai pas – *I haven't / I don't have*
je n'ai pas de – *I don't have any*
le temps (de...) – *the time (to...)*
avec moi – *with me*
je n'ai pas réservé – *I haven't reserved/booked*
apporter – *(to) bring*

How would you say these sentences in French?

What can I bring with me?

I'm going to bring it tomorrow.

Is it possible for you to bring it with you?

I'm not going to bring everything with me because it's too much.

I'm going to bring lots of things to eat.

What can I bring with me?
Que puis-je apporter avec moi?

I'm going to bring it tomorrow.
Je vais l'apporter demain.

Is it possible for you to bring it with you?
Est-ce que c'est possible pour vous de l'apporter avec vous?

I'm not going to bring everything with me because it's too much.
Je ne vais pas apporter tout avec moi parce que c'est trop.

I'm going to bring lots of things to eat.
Je vais apporter beaucoup de choses à manger.

You can change the verb "apporter" a little and get this phrase:

j'ai apporté

It means "I have brought"
You pronounce it "jshay ah-poor-TAY"

WORD LIST SO FAR

parce que – *because*
je n'ai pas – *I haven't / I don't have*
je n'ai pas de – *I don't have any*
le temps (de…) – *the time (to…)*
avec moi – *with me*
je n'ai pas réservé – *I haven't reserved/booked*
apporter – *(to) bring*
j'ai apporté – *I have brought*

How would you say these sentences in French?

I've brought something with me for you.

I've brought the wine but I don't have any food.

I've brought something with me for you.
J'ai apporté quelque chose avec moi pour vous.

I've brought the wine but I don't have any food.
J'ai apporté le vin mais je n'ai pas de nourriture.

We can change the phrase "j'ai apporté" a little to make the negative:

je n'ai pas apporté

It means "I haven't brought"
You pronounce it "jsheugh nay pah zah-poor-TAY"

WORD LIST SO FAR

parce que – *because*
je n'ai pas – *I haven't / I don't have*
je n'ai pas de – *I don't have any*
le temps (de…) – *the time (to…)*
avec moi – *with me*
je n'ai pas réservé – *I haven't reserved/booked*
apporter – *(to) bring*
j'ai apporté – *I have brought*
je n'ai pas apporté – *I haven't brought*

How would you say these sentences in French?

I haven't brought my passport.

I haven't brought my key with me.

I have brought some wine but I haven't brought any food.

I haven't brought my passport.
Je n'ai pas apporté mon passeport.

I haven't brought my key with me.
Je n'ai pas apporté ma clé avec moi.

I have brought some wine but I haven't brought any food.
J'ai apporté du vin mais je n'ai pas apporté de nourriture.

WORD LIST SO FAR

parce que – *because*
je n'ai pas – *I haven't / I don't have*
je n'ai pas de – *I don't have any*
le temps (de...) – *the time (to...)*
avec moi – *with me*
je n'ai pas réservé – *I haven't reserved/booked*
apporter – *(to) bring*
j'ai apporté – *I have brought*
je n'ai pas apporté – *I haven't brought*

It's time to practise what we've learnt in this lesson.

1. I haven't reserved a table because this restaurant isn't very busy
2. I don't have any wine at my house but I'm going to buy a bottle today
3. I have my car with me
4. Are you going to bring some food to Pierre's house?
5. I have brought something with me for you
6. I don't have the time to go with you today, but can I go tomorrow?
7. Do you have the time to make a reservation at the restaurant?
8. Do you have the time to buy something for Marie?
9. I didn't book a table but the restaurant isn't too busy
10. I didn't book but I would like a room for two people, if it's possible

1. Je n'ai pas réservé une table parce que ce restaurant n'est pas très occupé
2. Je n'ai pas de vin chez moi mais je vais acheter une bouteille aujourd'hui
3. J'ai ma voiture avec moi
4. Allez-vous apporter de la nourriture chez Pierre?
5. J'ai apporté quelque chose avec moi pour vous
6. Je n'ai pas le temps d'aller avec vous aujourd'hui, mais puis-je aller demain?
7. Avez-vous le temps de faire une réservation au restaurant?
8. Avez-vous le temps d'acheter quelque chose pour Marie?
9. Je n'ai pas réservé une table mais le restaurant n'est pas trop occupé
10. Je n'ai pas réservé mais je voudrais une chambre pour deux personnes, si c'est possible

Now, let's have a go at doing some reverse translations. Again, write down the English translations of the following French sentences, then check to see if you were correct.

1. Je n'ai pas le temps parce que je vais à Paris demain
2. Allez-vous apporter les billets demain?
3. Je n'ai pas mon passeport avec moi
4. Allez-vous apporter tout demain?
5. Pierre n'est pas ici aujourd'hui parce qu'il est trop occupé
6. Est-ce que c'est possible pour vous d'apporter encore une bouteille de ce vin pour moi?
7. Que puis-je apporter avec moi à l'hôtel?
8. Puis-je apporter mes amis avec moi aujourd'hui?
9. Voulez-vous aller au cinéma avec moi demain?
10. Je n'ai pas d'argent avec moi

1. I don't have the time because I'm going to Paris tomorrow
2. Are you going to bring the tickets tomorrow?
3. I don't have my passport with me
4. Are you going to bring everything tomorrow?
5. Pierre isn't here today because he's too busy
6. Is it possible for you to bring another bottle of this wine for me?
7. What can I bring with me to the hotel?
8. Can I bring my friends with me today?
9. Do you want to go to the cinema with me tomorrow?
10. I don't have any money with me

What we're going to do now are some recap translations, which will incorporate words we learnt in the previous lesson.

1. I like it in plastic
2. It's a bit too small for me
3. I would like to go to the butcher but it's too far from here and I don't have a car
4. What time are you going to Christine's house?
5. I think the restaurant is fantastic
6. It's quarter to eleven
7. It's three hundred and twenty euros for two weeks
8. Excuse me, how much is the wine here?
9. Hello, I am Pierre and I'd like a table for two, please
10. Marie is very tired

1. Je l'aime en plastique
2. C'est un peu trop petit pour moi
3. Je voudrais aller à la boucherie mais c'est trop loin d'ici et je n'ai pas de voiture
4. À quelle heure allez-vous chez Christine?
5. Pour moi, le restaurant est fantastique
6. Il est onze heures moins le quart
7. C'est trois cent vingt euros pour deux semaines
8. Excusez-moi, c'est combien le vin ici?
9. Bonjour, je suis Pierre et je voudrais une table pour deux, s'il vous plaît
10. Marie est très fatiguée

Let's now do some French to English recap translations. Grab a piece of paper and see if you can work out what these sentences mean.

1. Où est madame Petit?
2. Est-il pressé?
3. Non, je ne suis pas fatigué mais je suis très occupé
4. Ma réservation est sous le nom de Boulot
5. Allez-vous changer la réservation?
6. Je vais à la plage plus tard
7. Qu'allez-vous boire?
8. J'ai commandé une bouteille de vin
9. Voulez-vous encore la même chose?
10. Je ne me sens pas fantastique mais je ne me sens pas terrible

1. Where is Mrs Petit?
2. Is he in a hurry?
3. No, I'm not tired but I'm very busy
4. My reservation is in the name of Boulot
5. Are you going to change the reservation?
6. I'm going to the beach later
7. What are you going to drink?
8. I've ordered a bottle of wine
9. Do you want the same thing again?
10. I don't feel fantastic but I don't feel terrible

Let's recap all the words we've learnt so far. How did you say these words in French?

1. another (a different type)
2. (to) order
3. (to) change (exchange)
4. how
5. possible for me to...
6. the flu
7. for you
8. I haven't / I don't have
9. the same thing as him
10. something French
11. I haven't reserved / booked
12. no problem
13. a lot of
14. too much noise
15. (to) see
16. is he?
17. another (the same type) / again
18. he is
19. far from here
20. fine / well
21. I have brought
22. it wasn't
23. I'm not
24. I've hurt my...
25. expensive
26. near here
27. in a hurry
28. busy
29. the same thing as Pierre
30. (to) change it
31. I've caught
32. she isn't
33. (to) buy it
34. I'm doing well
35. something + adjective
36. later
37. is there? / are there?
38. my mum
39. tired
40. a postcard
41. are you going?
42. Mrs
43. wasn't
44. the same thing
45. the same thing as her
46. (to) try it
47. the same thing as you
48. what
49. (to) bring

50. I feel
51. Miss
52. a souvenir
53. today
54. I'm going
55. some/any medicine
56. something good
57. he isn't
58. (to) buy
59. Mr
60. I ordered
61. far
62. too many people
63. in the name of
64. I'm called
65. the same thing as me
66. I ate / I've eaten
67. I have reserved / I have booked
68. it was
69. is it...?
70. (to) change (modify)
71. I haven't brought
72. possible (to...)
73. because
74. yesterday
75. something from the region
76. a problem
77. things to...
78. I don't feel

79. if it's possible
80. is she?
81. (to) make/do it
82. do you want?
83. the time (to...)
84. too many cockroaches
85. I am
86. there is / there are
87. a cold
88. interesting
89. I have
90. was
91. ill
92. (to) eat
93. she is
94. with me
95. some stamps / any stamps
96. in the room
97. I've broken my...
98. something
99. now
100. too much... / too many...
101. are you?
102. (to) drink
103. there isn't any... / there aren't any...
104. how are you?
105. I'm not going

1. un/une autre
2. commander
3. changer de
4. comment
5. possible pour moi de...
6. la grippe
7. pour vous
8. je n'ai pas
9. la même chose que lui
10. quelque chose de français
11. je n'ai pas réservé
12. pas de problème
13. beaucoup de
14. trop de bruit
15. voir
16. est-il?
17. encore
18. il est
19. loin d'ici
20. bien
21. j'ai apporté
22. ce n'était pas
23. je ne suis pas
24. j'ai mal à...
25. cher
26. près d'ici
27. pressé
28. occupé
29. la même chose que Pierre
30. le changer
31. j'ai attrapé
32. elle n'est pas
33. l'acheter
34. je vais bien
35. quelque chose de + adjective
36. plus tard
37. y a-t-il?
38. ma mère
39. fatigué
40. une carte postale
41. allez-vous?
42. madame (Mme.)
43. n'était pas
44. la même chose
45. la même chose qu'elle
46. l'essayer
47. la même chose que vous
48. que
49. apporter
50. je me sens
51. mademoiselle (Mlle)
52. un souvenir
53. aujourd'hui
54. je vais
55. un médicament
56. quelque chose de bon
57. il n'est pas
58. acheter

59. monsieur (M.)
60. j'ai commandé
61. loin
62. trop de monde / trop de personnes
63. sous le nom de
64. je m'appelle
65. la même chose que moi
66. j'ai mangé
67. j'ai réservé
68. c'était
69. est-ce que c'est...?
70. changer
71. je n'ai pas apporté
72. possible (de...)
73. parce que
74. hier
75. quelque chose de la région
76. un problème
77. choses à...
78. je ne me sens pas
79. si c'est possible
80. est-elle?
81. le faire
82. voulez-vous?
83. le temps (de...)
84. trop de cafards
85. je suis
86. il y a
87. un rhume
88. intéressant
89. j'ai
90. était
91. malade
92. manger
93. elle est
94. avec moi
95. des timbres
96. dans la chambre
97. je me suis cassé...
98. quelque chose
99. maintenant
100. trop de...
101. êtes-vous?
102. boire
103. il n'y a pas de...
104. comment allez-vous?
105. je ne vais pas

LESSON 43

Let's start this lesson with a quick recap of the words and phrases we learnt in the last lesson. How do you say the following in French?

because
I haven't / I don't have
I don't have any
the time (to…)
with me
I haven't reserved
(to) bring
I have brought
I haven't brought

If there are any words you can't remember, go back to the last lesson and have a quick review of them before you start this lesson. It's really important that you remember the words you've learnt so far before you move on to learn any more.

Now, in this lesson, we're going to learn a bit of grammar...

The Past Tense

The past tense in French is fairly easy. There are two parts. Here is an example with the names for each part :

[1]J'ai [2]mangé
[1]I have [2]eaten

[1]J'AI	[2]MANGÉ
AUXILIARY VERB .	PAST PARTICIPLE .
I HAVE	EATEN

You can change the word "mangé" (the past participle) to any verb you like and change the meaning of the sentence.

j'ai **MANGÉ** – I have **EATEN**
j'ai **COMMANDÉ** – I have **ORDERED**
j'ai **RÉSERVÉ** – I have **RESERVED**
j'ai **CHANGÉ** – I have **CHANGED**

You've probably noticed that all the past participles end in the letter é with an accent on it. This is something you'll see a lot of in the past tense.

Forming the past participle

STEP 1: Remove the -er from the end of the verb
STEP 2: Put -é on the end instead

Par exemple (for example)

MANGER – MANGÉ
to eat – eaten

COMMANDER – COMMANDÉ
to order – ordered

RÉSERVER – RÉSERVÉ
to reserve – reserved

So, you always change the -er on the end of any infinitive to an -é in order to turn it into the past participle.

STEP 1: Remove the -er from the end of the verb
STEP 2: Put -é on the end instead

Try changing these verbs into the past participle. The answers are on the next page:

1. manger (to eat)
2. passer (to spend)
3. réserver (to reserve)
4. apporter (to bring)
5. oublier (to forget)

Here are the answers:

1. mangé (eaten)
2. passé (spent)
3. réservé (reserved)
4. apporté (brought)
5. oublié (forgotten)

All you have to do is put "j'ai" in front of those past participles to form a sentence in the past tense.

How would you say these sentences in French?

I have ordered.

I have eaten.

I have reserved.

I have ordered.
J'ai commandé.

I have eaten.
J'ai mangé.

I have reserved.
J'ai réservé.

Changing the auxiliary

Instead of saying "I have" all the time, you can change the sentence by changing the auxiliary verb (the "j'ai" part).

J'AI	I HAVE
TU AS	YOU HAVE
IL A	HE HAS
ELLE A	SHE HAS
PIERRE A	PIERRE HAS
NOUS AVONS	WE HAVE
VOUS AVEZ	YOU HAVE
ILS ONT	THEY HAVE

Have you seen that there are two ways to say "you" in French? "Tu" and "vous". Turn over to find out more...

You or you?

In French, there are two different ways to say "you".

We've already had "vous" and have been using that one for everything so far. However, there is also the word "tu".

"Tu" is used only when you're talking to one person whom you know very well. So, if it's a friend of yours, you can use "tu". In olden English, we used to have the word "thou" that was used with friends. For everything else, you use "vous".

So, unless you're talking to one person you know very well, then use "vous". (You should even use "vous" if you're talking to two people you know very well).

The proper words for these are formal, informal, singular and plural.

TU
singular informal

VOUS
singular formal / plural formal / plural informal

If in doubt, use "vous" and you won't go wrong.

So, how would you say these sentences in French?

I have eaten.

You have eaten.

He has eaten.

She has eaten.

Pierre has eaten.

Marie has eaten.

We have eaten.

They have eaten.

I have eaten.
J'ai mangé.

You have eaten.
Tu as mangé. / Vous avez mangé.

He has eaten.
Il a mangé.

She has eaten.
Elle a mangé.

Pierre has eaten.
Pierre a mangé.

Marie has eaten.
Marie a mangé.

We have eaten.
Nous avons mangé.

They have eaten.
Ils ont mangé.

ER becomes É

So far, we've learnt that you need to change the -er on the end of the verbs to an -é to make the past participle.

MANGER – MANGÉ
to eat – eaten

But, can you remember when I said a few lessons ago that there are different types of verbs in French? There are three different types, to be more specific, and it is all based on what letters they end in, either '**er**', '**ir**' or '**re**'.

What this means is that there are three different ways to make the past participle of a French verb. The three things to remember are:

ER *becomes* **É**
IR *becomes* **I**
RE *becomes* **U**

Forming the past participle

All you have to do to turn any verb into a past participle is to change the last two letters of the verb. If the verb ends in "er", change it to "é". If the verb ends in "ir", change it to an "i". If the verb ends in "re", change it to a "u".

ER *becomes* **É**
IR *becomes* **I**
RE *becomes* **U**

Par exemple (for example)

MANGER – MANGÉ
to eat – eaten

FINIR – FINI
to finish – finished

ATTENDRE – ATTENDU
to wait – waited

How would you say these sentences in French?

1. I have eaten.
2. You have eaten.
3. He has eaten.
4. She has eaten.
5. Pierre has eaten.
6. Marie has eaten.
7. We have eaten.
8. They have eaten.
9. I waited.
10. You waited.
11. He waited.
12. She waited.
13. Pierre waited.
14. Marie waited.
15. We waited.
16. They waited.
17. I have finished.
18. You have finished.
19. He has finished.
20. She has finished.
21. Pierre has finished.
22. Marie has finished.
23. We have finished.
24. They have finished.

1. J'ai mangé.
2. Tu as mangé. / Vous avez mangé.
3. Il a mangé.
4. Elle a mangé.
5. Pierre a mangé.
6. Marie a mangé.
7. Nous avons mangé.
8. Ils ont mangé.
9. J'ai attendu.
10. Tu as attendu. / Vous avez attendu.
11. Il a attendu.
12. Elle a attendu.
13. Pierre a attendu.
14. Marie a attendu.
15. Nous avons attendu.
16. Ils ont attendu.
17. J'ai fini.
18. Tu as fini. / Vous avez fini.
19. Il a fini.
20. Elle a fini.
21. Pierre a fini.
22. Marie a fini.
23. Nous avons fini.
24. Ils ont fini.

ER, IR, RE

So, you know there are three types of verb (ir, er, re) and you know how each one changes in the past. Here are a few verbs you can add to your vocabulary. On the left is the infinitive, and on the right is the past participle.

apporter - apporté
to bring - brought

réserver - réservé
to reserve - reserved

oublier - oublié
to forget - forgotten

perdre - perdu
to lose - lost

vendre - vendu
to sell - sold

attendre - attendu
to wait - waited

finir - fini
to finish - finished

choisir - choisi
to choose - chosen

ER *becomes* É
IR *becomes* I
RE *becomes* U

How would you say these sentences in French?

I have reserved a table.

I have brought Pierre.

I have forgotten.

I have chosen.

I have finished.

I have reserved a table.
J'ai réservé une table.

I have brought Pierre.
J'ai apporté Pierre.

I have forgotten.
J'ai oublié.

I have chosen.
J'ai choisi.

I have finished.
J'ai fini.

How would you say these sentences in French?

I have lost the car.

I have sold the car.

Pierre reserved a table yesterday.

Marie has brought some food with her.

They have forgotten everything.

I have lost the car.
J'ai perdu la voiture.

I have sold the car.
J'ai vendu la voiture.

Pierre reserved a table yesterday.
Pierre a réservé une table hier.

Marie has brought some food with her.
Marie a apporté de la nourriture avec elle.

They have forgotten everything.
Ils ont oublié tout.

How would you say these sentences in French?

She chose the red wine.

You have finished now.

We have lost the key.

She has sold the house.

She chose the red wine.
Elle a choisi le vin rouge.

You have finished now.
Tu as fini maintenant. /
Vous avez fini maintenant.

We have lost the key.
Nous avons perdu la clé.

She has sold the house.
Elle a vendu la maison.

Irregulars

Now, although most of the verbs in French follow the normal rule for changing into the past participle, there are a few verbs which do their own thing. So, here are some verbs that we call "irregular". Again, the infinitive is on the left and the past participle is on the right. These verbs don't follow the "er – é", "ir – i" or "re – u" rules.

boire - bu
to drink - drunk

faire - fait
to make / to do - made / done

voir - vu
to see - seen

prendre - pris
to take - taken

apprendre - appris
to learn - learned

comprendre - compris
to understand - understood

IRREGULAR VERBS

boire/bu – *to drink/drunk*

faire/fait – *to do/done – to make/made*

voir/vu – *to see/seen*

prendre/pris – *to take/taken*

apprendre/appris – *to learn/learned*

comprendre/compris – *to understand/understood*

How would you say these sentences in French?

I have drunk.

I have done.

I have seen Pierre.

I have taken.

I have learned.

I have understood.

I have drunk.
J'ai bu.

I have done.
J'ai fait.

I have seen Pierre.
J'ai vu Pierre.

I have taken.
J'ai pris.

I have learned.
J'ai appris.

I have understood.
J'ai compris.

How would you say these sentences in French?

He drank too much wine.

She has done everything today.

They saw the Eiffel Tower.

We took the car with us.

He learnt French.

She understood Michel very well.

He drank too much wine.
Il a bu trop de vin.

She has done everything today.
Elle a fait tout aujourd'hui.

They saw the Eiffel Tower.
Ils ont vu la Tour Eiffel.

We took the car with us.
Nous avons pris la voiture avec nous.

He learnt French.
Il a appris le français.

She understood Michel very well.
Elle a compris Michel très bien.

Talking about the past

So, here's a recap of the past tense before I let you loose on some translations.

STEP 1: Use an auxiliary verb

J'AI
I HAVE

STEP 2: Add the past participle

MANGÉ
EATEN

WORD LIST SO FAR

VERBS
apporter/apporté – *to bring/brought*
oublier/oublié – *to forget/forgotten*
perdre/perdu – *to lose/lost*
vendre/vendu – *to sell/sold*
attendre/attendu – *to wait/waited*
finir/fini – *to finish/finished*
choisir/choisi – *to choose/chosen*

AUXILIARY VERBS
j'ai – *I have*
tu as – *you have*
il a – *he has*
elle a – *she has*
Pierre a – *Pierre has*
nous avons – *we have*
vous avez – *you have*
ils ont – *they have*

PAST PARTICIPLE
er - é
ir - i
re - u

IRREGULAR VERBS

boire/bu – *to drink/drunk*

faire/fait – *to do/done – to make/made*

voir/vu – *to see/seen*

prendre/pris – *to take/taken*

apprendre/appris – *to learn/learned*

comprendre/compris – *to understand/understood*

It's time to practise what we've learnt in this lesson.

Grab a piece of paper and see if you can write down the following sentences in French. Then, you can check the answers.

1. Pierre is tired because he drank too much wine
2. We have sold the car because it was too expensive
3. I waited here yesterday
4. They finished before me
5. Marie chose the red wine but I chose the white wine
6. You forgot the cheese!
7. I lost my passport in my room
8. I understood everything very well but Pierre didn't understand
9. I made a cake for you
10. I learnt French because I would like to go to Paris

1. Pierre est fatigué parce qu'il a bu trop de vin
2. Nous avons vendu la voiture parce qu'elle était trop chère
3. J'ai attendu ici hier
4. Ils ont fini avant moi
5. Marie a choisi le vin rouge mais j'ai choisi le vin blanc
6. Vous avez / Tu as oublié le fromage!
7. J'ai perdu mon passeport dans ma chambre
8. J'ai compris tout très bien mais Pierre n'a pas compris
9. J'ai fait un gâteau pour vous
10. J'ai appris le français parce que je voudrais aller à Paris

Now, let's have a go at doing some reverse translations. Again, write down the English translations of the following French sentences, then check to see if you were correct.

1. Il a vu la Tour Eiffel en France
2. Elle a pris les billets avec elle
3. Vous avez / Tu as apporté le vin et j'ai apporté la nourriture
4. Ils ont oublié les billets pour le train
5. J'ai pris tout avec moi hier
6. J'ai vu ce film et je l'aime beaucoup
7. Il a fait tout hier et elle a fait tout aujourd'hui
8. Nous avons appris ça
9. Marie a bu mon vin parce que je ne l'aime pas
10. Nous avons compris beaucoup mais pas tout

1. He saw the Eiffel Tower in France
2. She took the tickets with her
3. You brought the wine and I brought the food
4. They forgot the tickets for the train
5. I took everything with me yesterday
6. I've seen this film and I like it a lot
7. He did everything yesterday and she did everything today
8. We learnt that
9. Marie drank my wine because I don't like it
10. We understood a lot but not everything

What we're going to do now are some recap translations, which will incorporate words we learnt in the previous lessons.

1. I would like to buy dinner for you tonight
2. The food is delicious but everything is always very expensive here
3. Is there a good restaurant near here?
4. What is there for (the) children?
5. Do you want to try something different today?
6. Is that for me?
7. Is it possible for me to pay later?
8. There is a problem with the shower in my room
9. There are too many people here today
10. It's absolutely extraordinary here

1. Je voudrais acheter le dîner pour vous ce soir
2. La nourriture est délicieuse mais tout est toujours très cher ici
3. Y a-t-il un bon restaurant près d'ici?
4. Qu'y a-t-il pour les enfants?
5. Voulez-vous essayer quelque chose de différent aujourd'hui?
6. Est-ce que ça c'est pour moi?
7. Est-ce que c'est possible pour moi de payer plus tard?
8. Il y a un problème avec la douche dans ma chambre
9. Il y a trop de personnes ici aujourd'hui
10. C'est absolument extraordinaire ici

Let's now do some French to English recap translations. Grab a piece of paper and see if you can work out what these sentences mean.

1. Ce n'est pas mauvais mais ce n'est pas parfait
2. Ce n'est pas pour lui; c'est pour moi
3. Puis-je faire une réservation pour trois personnes, s'il vous plaît?
4. C'est combien pour trois jours?
5. Excusez-moi, où puis-je louer une voiture pour deux semaines?
6. Je voudrais aller à la plage demain
7. Puis-je aller avec Pierre chez Sophie plus tard?
8. Je voudrais payer par carte
9. Il est cinq heures
10. Une bouteille de vin rouge est huit euros cinquante

1. It isn't bad but it isn't perfect
2. It isn't for him; it's for me
3. Can I make a reservation for three people, please?
4. How much is it for three days?
5. Excuse me, where can I hire a car for two weeks?
6. I would like to go to the beach tomorrow
7. Can I go with Pierre to Sophie's house later?
8. I would like to pay by card
9. It's five o'clock
10. A bottle of red wine is eight euros fifty

Let's recap all the words we've learnt so far. How did you say these words in French?

1. he isn't
2. expensive
3. no problem
4. now
5. is he?
6. I am
7. the same thing as you
8. do you want?
9. (to) understand / understood
10. the time (to...)
11. I ordered
12. I've caught
13. in a hurry
14. fine / well
15. there is / there are
16. I ate / I've eaten
17. with me
18. I'm called
19. today
20. Miss
21. (to) see / seen
22. Mr
23. another (a different type)
24. I'm not going
25. the same thing as Pierre
26. I have reserved / I have booked
27. a cold
28. the same thing
29. (to) wait / waited
30. how
31. yesterday
32. (to) bring / brought
33. a problem
34. busy
35. Pierre has
36. it was
37. too many people
38. in the room
39. I have brought
40. (to) learn / learned
41. what
42. the same thing as him
43. (to) lose / lost
44. (to) drink
45. (to) see
46. I'm doing well
47. are you?

48. something + adjective
49. interesting
50. (to) make/do it
51. (to) bring
52. I haven't reserved / booked
53. (to) sell / sold
54. (to) change (modify)
55. there isn't any... / there aren't any...
56. ill
57. (to) do / done
58. too much noise
59. my mum
60. (to) buy
61. I've hurt my...
62. some/any medicine
63. too much... / too many...
64. possible for me to...
65. because
66. he has
67. I haven't brought
68. I don't feel
69. (to) order
70. she has
71. tired
72. I haven't / I don't have
73. something French
74. some stamps / any stamps
75. a souvenir
76. another (the same type) / again
77. (to) change (exchange)
78. something
79. I'm going
80. the flu
81. she is
82. a postcard
83. I've broken my...
84. (to) forget / forgotten
85. she isn't
86. (to) try it
87. I'm not
88. is there? / are there?
89. later
90. a lot of
91. you have
92. too many cockroaches
93. possible (to...)

94. was
95. the same thing as me
96. is she?
97. far
98. are you going?
99. it wasn't
100. in the name of
101. something good
102. how are you?
103. (to) change it
104. (to) choose / chosen
105. we have
106. I feel
107. (to) take / taken
108. (to) drink / drunk
109. (to) eat
110. I have
111. (to) finish / finished
112. for you
113. he is
114. they have
115. things to...
116. far from here
117. something from the region
118. the same thing as her
119. (to) make / made
120. wasn't
121. (to) buy it
122. near here
123. if it's possible
124. Mrs
125. is it...?

1. il n'est pas
2. cher
3. pas de problème
4. maintenant
5. est-il?
6. je suis
7. la même chose que vous
8. voulez-vous?
9. comprendre / compris
10. le temps (de...)
11. j'ai commandé
12. j'ai attrapé
13. pressé
14. bien
15. il y a
16. j'ai mangé
17. avec moi
18. je m'appelle
19. aujourd'hui
20. mademoiselle (Mlle)
21. voir / vu
22. monsieur (M.)
23. un/une autre
24. je ne vais pas
25. la même chose que Pierre
26. j'ai réservé
27. un rhume
28. la même chose
29. attendre / attendu
30. comment
31. hier
32. apporter / apporté
33. un problème
34. occupé
35. Pierre a
36. c'était
37. trop de monde / trop de personnes
38. dans la chambre
39. j'ai apporté
40. apprendre / appris
41. que
42. la même chose que lui
43. perdre / perdu
44. boire
45. voir
46. je vais bien
47. êtes-vous?
48. quelque chose de + adjective
49. intéressant
50. le faire
51. apporter
52. je n'ai pas réservé
53. vendre / vendu
54. changer
55. il n'y a pas de...
56. malade
57. faire / fait
58. trop de bruit
59. ma mère
60. acheter

61. j'ai mal à...
62. un médicament
63. trop de...
64. possible pour moi de...
65. parce que
66. il a
67. je n'ai pas apporté
68. je ne me sens pas
69. commander
70. elle a
71. fatigué
72. je n'ai pas
73. quelque chose de français
74. des timbres
75. un souvenir
76. encore
77. changer de
78. quelque chose
79. je vais
80. la grippe
81. elle est
82. une carte postale
83. je me suis cassé...
84. oublier / oublié
85. elle n'est pas
86. l'essayer
87. je ne suis pas
88. y a-t-il?
89. plus tard
90. beaucoup de
91. vous avez / tu as
92. trop de cafards

93. possible (de...)
94. était
95. la même chose que moi
96. est-elle?
97. loin
98. allez-vous?
99. ce n'était pas
100. sous le nom de
101. quelque chose de bon
102. comment allez-vous?
103. le changer
104. choisir / choisi
105. nous avons
106. je me sens
107. prendre / pris
108. boire / bu
109. manger
110. j'ai
111. finir / fini
112. pour vous
113. il est
114. ils ont
115. choses à...
116. loin d'ici
117. quelque chose de la région
118. la même chose qu'elle
119. faire / fait
120. n'était pas
121. l'acheter

LESSON 43 ½

Now, this is just a quick lesson to talk about a little problem that appears in English, not in French...

The Past Tense

So, we've learnt so far that the past tense in French is made up of two different parts :

¹J'ai ²mangé
¹I have ²eaten

¹J'AI	²MANGÉ
AUXILIARY VERB .	PAST PARTICIPLE .
I HAVE	EATEN

This is all fine and dandy, but, in English, we have two ways to talk about the past. You can say either

I have eaten

or

I ate

Thankfully, in French, there is only the one version, so no matter whether you want to say "I have eaten" or "I ate", in French, it's always just "j'ai mangé".

In English, the "I ate" version is called the "simple past" and the "I have eaten" version is called the "present perfect". In French, the simple past doesn't exist, they only have the present perfect tense (even though it has the word "present" in it, it is actually a past tense).

So, keeping in mind that there is only one way to talk about the past in French, how would you say these?

1. I have eaten
2. I ate
3. You have eaten
4. You ate
5. He has eaten
6. He ate
7. She has eaten
8. She ate
9. Pierre has eaten
10. Pierre ate
11. Marie has eaten
12. Marie ate
13. We have eaten
14. We ate
15. They have eaten
16. They ate
17. I have waited
18. I waited
19. You have waited
20. You waited
21. He has waited
22. He waited
23. She has waited
24. She waited
25. Pierre has waited
26. Pierre waited
27. Marie has waited

28. Marie waited
29. We have waited
30. We waited
31. They have waited
32. They waited
33. I have finished
34. I finished
35. You have finished
36. You finished
37. He has finished
38. He finished
39. She has finished
40. She finished
41. Pierre has finished
42. Pierre finished
43. Marie has finished
44. Marie finished
45. We have finished
46. We finished
47. They have finished
48. They finished
49. I have reserved a table
50. I reserved a table
51. I have brought Pierre with me
52. I brought Pierre with me
53. I have forgotten
54. I forgot
55. I have chosen
56. I chose
57. I have finished
58. I finished

59. I have lost the car
60. I lost the car
61. I have sold the car
62. I sold the car
63. I have drunk
64. I drank
65. I have done
66. I did
67. I have seen Pierre
68. I saw Pierre
69. I have taken
70. I took
71. I have learnt
72. I learnt
73. I have understood
74. I understood

Here are the answers:

1. J'ai mangé
2. J'ai mangé
3. Tu as mangé / vous avez mangé
4. Tu as mangé / vous avez mangé
5. Il a mangé
6. Il a mangé
7. Elle a mangé
8. Elle a mangé
9. Pierre a mangé
10. Pierre mangé
11. Marie a mangé
12. Marie a mangé
13. Nous avons mangé
14. Nous avons mangé
15. Ils ont mangé
16. Ils ont mangé
17. J'ai attendu
18. J'ai attendu
19. Tu as attendu / vous avez attendu
20. Tu as attendu / vous avez attendu
21. Il a attendu
22. Il a attendu
23. Elle a attendu
24. Elle a attendu
25. Pierre a attendu
26. Pierre a attendu
27. Marie a attendu
28. Marie a attendu
29. Nous avons attendu

30. Nous avons attendu
31. Ils ont attendu
32. Ils ont attendu
33. J'ai fini
34. J'ai fini
35. Tu as fini / vous avez fini
36. Tu as fini / vous avez fini
37. Il a fini
38. Il a fini
39. Elle a fini
40. Elle a fini
41. Pierre a fini
42. Pierre a fini
43. Marie a fini
44. Marie a fini
45. Nous avons fini
46. Nous avons fini
47. Ils ont fini
48. Ils ont fini
49. J'ai réservé une table
50. J'ai réservé une table
51. J'ai apporté Pierre avec moi
52. J'ai apporté Pierre avec moi
53. J'ai oublié
54. J'ai oublié
55. J'ai choisi
56. J'ai choisi
57. J'ai fini
58. J'ai fini
59. J'ai perdu la voiture
60. J'ai perdu la voiture

61. J'ai vendu la voiture
62. J'ai vendu la voiture
63. J'ai bu
64. J'ai bu
65. J'ai fait
66. J'ai fait
67. J'ai vu Pierre
68. J'ai vu Pierre
69. J'ai pris
70. J'ai pris
71. J'ai appris
72. J'ai appris
73. J'ai compris
74. J'ai compris

LESSON 44

Let's start this lesson with a quick recap of the words and phrases we learnt in the last lesson. How do you say the following in French?

to bring / brought
to forget / forgotten
to lose / lost
to sell / sold
to wait / waited
to finish / finished
to choose / chosen
to drink / drunk
to do/make / done/made
to see / seen
to take / taken
to learn / learnt
to understand / understood
I have
you have
he has
she has
Pierre has
we have
they have

In this lesson, we'll add a little extra to the past tense

The Negative Past Tense

So, in the last lesson, we learnt how the past was made up of two parts :

$$^1J'ai \ ^2mangé$$
$$^1I \ have \ ^2eaten$$

¹J'AI	²MANGÉ
AUXILIARY VERB .	PAST PARTICIPLE .
I HAVE	EATEN

But, what if you want to say that you haven't eaten? Well, all you do is change the auxiliary verb slightly to make it negative.

[1]Je n'ai pas [2]mangé
[1]I haven't [2]eaten

[1]JE N'AI PAS	[2]MANGÉ
NEGATIVE AUXILIARY VERB .	PAST PARTICIPLE .
I HAVEN'T	EATEN

So, "je n'ai pas" means "I haven't". Therefore, how would you say these sentences in French?

I haven't ordered.

I haven't eaten.

I haven't reserved.

I haven't ordered.
Je n'ai pas commandé.

I haven't eaten.
Je n'ai pas mangé.

I haven't reserved.
Je n'ai pas réservé.

Changing the auxiliary

Can you remember all the different versions of the auxiliary verbs from the last lesson?

J'AI	I HAVE
TU AS	YOU HAVE
IL A	HE HAS
ELLE A	SHE HAS
PIERRE A	PIERRE HAS
NOUS AVONS	WE HAVE
VOUS AVEZ	YOU HAVE
ILS ONT	THEY HAVE

Well, as you've seen, to change "I have" to "I haven't" in French, you simply have to put a n'...pas around the "have" part:

J'AI - JE N'AI PAS
I have - I haven't

You can do the same to change any of the auxiliaries into their negative versions, For example:

IL A - IL N'A PAS
he has - he hasn't

WORD LIST SO FAR

je n'ai pas – *I haven't*
il n'a pas – *he hasn't*

How would you say these sentences in French?

He hasn't ordered.

He hasn't eaten.

He hasn't reserved.

He hasn't ordered.
Il n'a pas commandé.

He hasn't eaten.
Il n'a pas mangé.

He hasn't reserved.
Il n'a pas réservé.

The Negative Auxiliary

Here is the entire list of the negative conjugation for the auxiliary verb:

JE N'AI PAS	I HAVEN'T
TU N'AS PAS	YOU HAVEN'T
IL N'A PAS	HE HASN'T
ELLE N'A PAS	SHE HASN'T
PIERRE N'A PAS	PIERRE HASN'T
NOUS N'AVONS PAS	WE HAVEN'T
VOUS N'AVEZ PAS	YOU HAVEN'T
ILS N'ONT PAS	THEY HAVEN'T

WORD LIST SO FAR

je n'ai pas – *I haven't*
tu n'as pas / vous n'avez pas – *You haven't*
il n'a pas – *he hasn't*
elle n'a pas – *she hasn't*
Pierre n'a pas – *Pierre hasn't*
nous n'avons pas – *we haven't*
ils n'ont pas – *they haven't*

How would you say these sentences in French?

I haven't eaten.

You haven't eaten.

He hasn't eaten.

She hasn't eaten.

Pierre hasn't eaten.

Marie hasn't eaten.

We haven't eaten.

They haven't eaten.

I haven't eaten.
Je n'ai pas mangé.

You haven't eaten.
**Tu n'as pas mangé. /
Vous n'avez pas mangé.**

He hasn't eaten.
Il n'a pas mangé.

She hasn't eaten.
Elle n'a pas mangé.

Pierre hasn't eaten.
Pierre n'a pas mangé.

Marie hasn't eaten.
Marie n'a pas mangé.

We haven't eaten.
Nous n'avons pas mangé.

They haven't eaten.
Ils n'ont pas mangé.

See if you can put these sentences into French.
The answers are on the next page:

1. I haven't waited
2. You haven't waited
3. He hasn't waited
4. She hasn't waited
5. Pierre hasn't waited
6. Marie hasn't waited
7. We haven't waited
8. They haven't waited
9. I haven't finished
10. You haven't finished
11. He hasn't finished
12. She hasn't finished
13. Pierre hasn't finished
14. Marie hasn't finished
15. We haven't finished
16. They haven't finished

Here are the answers:

1. Je n'ai pas attendu
2. Tu n'as pas attendu / Vous n'avez pas attendu
3. Il n'a pas attendu
4. Elle n'a pas attendu
5. Pierre n'a pas attendu
6. Marie n'a pas attendu
7. Nous n'avons pas attendu
8. Ils n'ont pas attendu
9. Je n'ai pas fini
10. Tu n'as pas fini / Vous n'avez pas fini
11. Il n'a pas fini
12. Elle n'a pas fini
13. Pierre n'a pas fini
14. Marie n'a pas fini
15. Nous n'avons pas fini
16. Ils n'ont pas fini

WORD LIST SO FAR

je n'ai pas – *I haven't*
tu n'as pas / vous n'avez pas – *You haven't*
il n'a pas – *he hasn't*
elle n'a pas – *she hasn't*
Pierre n'a pas – *Pierre hasn't*
nous n'avons pas – *we haven't*
ils n'ont pas – *they haven't*

It's time to practise what we've learnt in this lesson.

Grab a piece of paper and see if you can write down the following sentences in French. Then, you can check the answers.

1. I haven't finished everything
2. He hasn't seen Marie today
3. Pierre hasn't eaten much (a lot) today because he is ill
4. They haven't brought any wine
5. We haven't seen this film, it's very good
6. You haven't drunk the coffee
7. He hasn't made a reservation
8. She hasn't booked a table for tomorrow
9. They haven't learnt English
10. Marie hasn't sold the car

1. Je n'ai pas fini tout
2. Il n'a pas vu Marie aujourd'hui
3. Pierre n'a pas mangé beaucoup aujourd'hui parce qu'il est malade
4. Ils n'ont pas apporté de vin
5. Nous n'avons pas vu ce film, c'est très bon
6. Tu n'as pas / Vous n'avez pas bu le café
7. Il n'a pas fait une réservation
8. Elle n'a pas réservé une table pour demain
9. Ils n'ont pas appris l'anglais
10. Marie n'a pas vendu la voiture

Now, let's have a go at doing some reverse translations. Again, write down the English translations of the following French sentences, then check to see if you were correct.

1. Je n'ai pas mangé beaucoup de nourriture aujourd'hui parce que je suis très occupé
2. Il n'a pas bu de vin
3. Je n'ai pas choisi mais j'aime ce vin rouge
4. Elle n'a pas pris la voiture; elle est là
5. Pierre n'a pas compris
6. Je n'ai pas perdu la voiture
7. Je n'ai pas oublié mon passeport mais je n'ai pas mes billets
8. Il n'a pas fait tout; Marie a fait beaucoup
9. Nous n'avons pas fait un gâteau parce que nous avons oublié
10. Je me sens très malade et je n'ai pas fait le dîner

1. I haven't eaten much (a lot of) food today because I'm very busy
2. He hasn't drunk any wine
3. I haven't chosen but I like this red wine
4. She hasn't taken the car; it's there
5. Pierre hasn't understood
6. I haven't lost the car
7. I haven't forgotten my passport but I don't have my tickets
8. He hasn't done everything; Marie did a lot
9. We haven't made a cake because we forgot
10. I feel very ill and I haven't made the dinner

What we're going to do now are some recap translations, which will incorporate words we learnt in the previous lesson.

1. The bill is fifty euros but I don't have any money with me
2. Can I try the carrots?
3. I'm going to take a taxi to the hotel because it's (he is) too far
4. Take the first road on the left and then the third road on the right
5. I think the restaurant is fantastic
6. I like the red coat but I prefer it in orange
7. Do you want to try my wine?
8. I think everybody is very nice
9. I've caught a terrible cold again
10. It's delicious, but is it good for me?

1. L'addition est cinquante euros mais je n'ai pas d'argent avec moi
2. Puis-je essayer les carottes?
3. Je vais prendre un taxi à l'hôtel parce qu'il est trop loin
4. Prenez la première rue à gauche et puis la troisième rue à droite
5. Pour moi, le restaurant est fantastique
6. J'aime le manteau rouge mais je le préfère en orange
7. Voulez-vous essayer mon vin?
8. Pour moi, tout le monde est très sympa
9. J'ai attrapé encore un rhume terrible
10. C'est délicieux, mais est-ce que c'est bon pour moi?

Let's now do some French to English recap translations. Grab a piece of paper and see if you can work out what these sentences mean.

1. Je voudrais encore deux bouteilles d'eau, s'il vous plaît
2. La clé pour ma chambre ne marche pas
3. Excusez-moi, où sont les chariots?
4. Le thé est pour lui et le café est pour moi
5. J'ai commandé le poulet pour moi mais je n'ai pas commandé pour vous
6. Je me suis cassé la jambe
7. J'ai une réservation sous le nom de Charles
8. Qu'allez-vous acheter pour Marie?
9. C'est combien l'addition?
10. Quels allez-vous choisir?

1. I would like another two bottles of water, please
2. The key for my room doesn't work
3. Excuse me, where are the trolleys?
4. The tea is for him and the coffee is for me
5. I've ordered the chicken for me but I haven't ordered for you
6. I've broken my leg
7. I have a reservation in the name of Charles
8. What are you going to buy for Marie?
9. How much is the bill?
10. Which ones are you going to choose?

Let's recap all the words we've learnt so far. How did you say these words in French?

1. (to) buy
2. (to) order
3. for you
4. a souvenir
5. what
6. too many cockroaches
7. possible (to...)
8. is there? / are there?
9. the time (to...)
10. I'm not going
11. with me
12. is he?
13. busy
14. possible for me to...
15. (to) lose / lost
16. he has
17. they haven't
18. (to) choose / chosen
19. (to) make/do it
20. I've broken my...
21. something French
22. are you going?
23. (to) see / seen
24. (to) do / done
25. (to) try it
26. because
27. ill
28. another (a different type)
29. (to) finish / finished
30. a postcard
31. something from the region
32. (to) make / made
33. a problem
34. Mr
35. later
36. near here
37. (to) change (modify)
38. the same thing as her
39. is she?
40. I have brought
41. I haven't / I don't have
42. (to) take / taken
43. they have
44. the same thing as him
45. too much noise
46. I'm not
47. something good
48. in the room
49. things to...
50. far
51. Pierre has

52. (to) forget / forgotten
53. the flu
54. she hasn't
55. something
56. another (the same type) / again
57. we haven't
58. I ordered
59. I've caught
60. some stamps / any stamps
61. it was
62. tired
63. (to) change (exchange)
64. Miss
65. no problem
66. in a hurry
67. (to) eat
68. the same thing as me
69. if it's possible
70. was
71. how are you?
72. the same thing as you
73. how
74. I'm doing well
75. a lot of
76. I haven't brought
77. (to) bring
78. you haven't
79. she isn't
80. wasn't
81. do you want?
82. I'm called
83. (to) sell / sold
84. in the name of
85. (to) understand / understood
86. I've hurt my...
87. some/any medicine
88. I have reserved / I have booked
89. Mrs
90. the same thing as Pierre
91. interesting
92. I ate / I've eaten
93. he is
94. I feel
95. too much... / too many...
96. a cold
97. something + adjective
98. are you?
99. (to) bring / brought
100. my mum
101. is it...?
102. far from here
103. yesterday
104. I'm going
105. you have
106. he hasn't
107. fine / well
108. the same thing

1. acheter
2. commander
3. pour vous
4. un souvenir
5. que
6. trop de cafards
7. possible (de...)
8. y a-t-il?
9. le temps (de...)
10. je ne vais pas
11. avec moi
12. est-il?
13. occupé
14. possible pour moi de...
15. perdre / perdu
16. il a
17. ils n'ont pas
18. choisir / choisi
19. le faire
20. je me suis cassé...
21. quelque chose de français
22. allez-vous?
23. voir / vu
24. faire / fait
25. l'essayer
26. parce que
27. malade
28. un/une autre
29. finir / fini
30. une carte postale
31. quelque chose de la région
32. faire / fait
33. un problème
34. monsieur (M.)
35. plus tard
36. près d'ici
37. changer
38. la même chose qu'elle
39. est-elle?
40. j'ai apporté
41. je n'ai pas
42. prendre / pris
43. ils ont
44. la même chose que lui
45. trop de bruit
46. je ne suis pas
47. quelque chose de bon
48. dans la chambre
49. choses à...
50. loin
51. Pierre a
52. oublier / oublié
53. la grippe
54. elle n'a pas
55. quelque chose
56. encore
57. nous n'avons pas
58. j'ai commandé
59. j'ai attrapé

60. des timbres
61. c'était
62. fatigué
63. changer de
64. mademoiselle (Mlle)
65. pas de problème
66. pressé
67. manger
68. la même chose que moi
69. si c'est possible
70. était
71. comment allez-vous?
72. la même chose que vous
73. comment
74. je vais bien
75. beaucoup de
76. je n'ai pas apporté
77. apporter
78. tu n'as pas / vous n'avez pas
79. elle n'est pas
80. n'était pas
81. voulez-vous?
82. je m'appelle
83. vendre / vendu
84. sous le nom de
85. comprendre / compris
86. j'ai mal à...
87. un médicament
88. j'ai réservé
89. madame (Mme.)
90. la même chose que Pierre
91. intéressant
92. j'ai mangé
93. il est
94. je me sens
95. trop de...
96. un rhume
97. quelque chose de + adjective
98. êtes-vous?
99. apporter / apporté
100. ma mère
101. est-ce que c'est...?
102. loin d'ici
103. hier
104. je vais
105. vous avez / tu as
106. il n'a pas
107. bien
108. la même chose
109. le changer
110. boire / bu
111. elle a
112. apprendre / appris
113. boire
114. l'acheter
115. aujourd'hui
116. il y a
117. maintenant
118. il n'y a pas de...
119. trop de monde / trop de personnes

120. je suis
121. Pierre n'a pas
122. voir
123. je n'ai pas réservé
124. elle est
125. ce n'était pas

126. j'ai
127. attendre / attendu
128. il n'est pas
129. cher
130. je ne me sens pas
131. nous avons

LESSON 44½

Now, this is just another quick lesson to talk about another little problem that exists in English but not in French.

The Negative Past Tense

¹JE N'AI PAS	²MANGÉ
NEGATIVE AUXILIARY VERB .	PAST PARTICIPLE .
I HAVEN'T	EATEN

So, hopefully, you've now grasped how to talk about the past in the negative. Again, this is all fine and dandy in French, but in English, we have two ways to talk about the negative past. You can either say :

I haven't eaten

or

I didn't eat

Thankfully, in French, there is only one version. Therefore, no matter whether you want to say "I haven't eaten" or "I didn't eat", it's always just "je n'ai pas mangé".

Je n'ai pas mangé
I haven't eaten / I didn't eat

See if you can put these sentences into French.
The answers are at the end:

1. I haven't eaten
2. I didn't eat
3. You haven't eaten
4. You didn't eat
5. He hasn't eaten
6. He didn't eat
7. She hasn't eaten
8. She didn't eat
9. Pierre hasn't eaten
10. Pierre didn't eat
11. Marie hasn't eaten
12. Marie didn't eat
13. We haven't eaten
14. We didn't eat
15. They haven't eaten
16. They didn't eat
17. I haven't waited
18. I didn't wait
19. You haven't waited
20. You didn't wait
21. He hasn't waited
22. He didn't wait
23. She hasn't waited
24. She didn't wait
25. Pierre hasn't waited
26. Pierre didn't wait
27. Marie hasn't waited
28. Marie didn't wait

29. We haven't waited
30. We didn't wait
31. They haven't waited
32. They didn't wait
33. I haven't finished
34. I didn't finish
35. You haven't finished
36. You didn't finish
37. He hasn't finished
38. He didn't finish
39. She hasn't finished
40. She didn't finish
41. Pierre hasn't finished
42. Pierre didn't finish
43. Marie hasn't finished
44. Marie didn't finish
45. We haven't finished
46. We didn't finish
47. They haven't finished
48. They didn't finish
49. I haven't reserved a table
50. I didn't reserve a table
51. I haven't brought Pierre
52. I didn't bring Pierre
53. I haven't forgotten
54. I didn't forget
55. I haven't chosen
56. I didn't choose
57. I haven't finished
58. I didn't finish
59. I haven't lost the car

60. I didn't lose the car
61. I haven't sold the car
62. I didn't sell the car
63. I haven't drunk
64. I didn't drink
65. I haven't done
66. I didn't do
67. I haven't seen Pierre
68. I didn't see Pierre
69. I haven't taken
70. I didn't take
71. I haven't learnt
72. I didn't learn
73. I haven't understood
74. I didn't understand

Here are the answers:

1. Je n'ai pas mangé
2. Je n'ai pas mangé
3. Tu n'as pas mangé / Vous n'avez pas mangé
4. Tu n'as pas mangé / Vous n'avez pas mangé
5. Il n'a pas mangé
6. Il n'a pas mangé
7. Elle n'a pas mangé
8. Elle n'a pas mangé
9. Pierre n'a pas mangé
10. Pierre n'a pas mangé
11. Marie n'a pas mangé
12. Marie n'a pas mangé
13. Nous n'avons pas mangé
14. Nous n'avons pas mangé
15. Ils n'ont pas mangé
16. Ils n'ont pas mangé
17. Je n'ai pas attendu
18. Je n'ai pas attendu
19. Tu n'as pas attendu / Vous n'avez pas attendu
20. Tu n'as pas attendu / Vous n'avez pas attendu
21. Il n'a pas attendu
22. Il n'a pas attendu
23. Elle n'a pas attendu
24. Elle n'a pas attendu
25. Pierre n'a pas attendu
26. Pierre n'a pas attendu
27. Marie n'a pas attendu
28. Marie n'a pas attendu
29. Nous n'avons pas attendu

30. Nous n'avons pas attendu
31. Ils n'ont pas attendu
32. Ils n'ont pas attendu
33. Je n'ai pas fini
34. Je n'ai pas fini
35. Tu n'as pas fini / Vous n'avez pas fini
36. Tu n'as pas fini / Vous n'avez pas fini
37. Il n'a pas fini
38. Il n'a pas fini
39. Elle n'a pas fini
40. Elle n'a pas fini
41. Pierre n'a pas fini
42. Pierre n'a pas fini
43. Marie n'a pas fini
44. Marie n'a pas fini
45. Nous n'avons pas fini
46. Nous n'avons pas fini
47. Ils n'ont pas fini
48. Ils n'ont pas fini
49. Je n'ai pas réservé une table
50. Je n'ai pas réservé une table
51. Je n'ai pas apporté Pierre
52. Je n'ai pas apporté Pierre
53. Je n'ai pas oublié
54. Je n'ai pas oublié
55. Je n'ai pas choisi
56. Je n'ai pas choisi
57. Je n'ai pas fini
58. Je n'ai pas fini
59. Je n'ai pas perdu la voiture
60. Je n'ai pas perdu la voiture

61. Je n'ai pas vendu la voiture

62. Je n'ai pas vendu la voiture

63. Je n'ai pas bu

64. Je n'ai pas bu

65. Je n'ai pas fait

66. Je n'ai pas fait

67. Je n'ai pas vu Pierre

68. Je n'ai pas vu Pierre

69. Je n'ai pas pris

70. Je n'ai pas pris

71. Je n'ai pas appris

72. Je n'ai pas appris

73. Je n'ai pas compris

74. Je n'ai pas compris

Vocabulary Expansion Section

La famille et les amis
Family and friends

la famille nucléaire	*the nuclear family*
ma mère	my mother
ma maman	my mum
mon père	my father
mon papa	my dad
mon frère	my brother
ma sœur	my sister
mes frères et sœurs	my siblings
mes parents	my parents
un parent isolé	a single parent
une mère célibataire	a single mother
un père célibataire	a single father
ma belle-mère	my stepmother
mon beau-père	my stepfather
le fils de mon beau-père	my stepbrother (son of stepfather)
le fils de ma belle-mère	my stepbrother (son of stepmother)

la fille de mon beau-père	my stepsister (daughter of stepfather)
la fille de ma belle-mère	my stepsister (daughter of stepmother)
mon demi-frère	my half brother
ma demi-sœur	my half sister
mon fils	my son
ma fille	my daughter
mon beau-fils	my stepson
ma belle-fille	my stepdaughter
mes enfants	my children
mon mari	my husband
ma femme	my wife
mon époux	my spouse (man)
mon épouse	my spouse (woman)
mon conjoint	my partner (man)
ma conjointe	my partner (woman)
mon petit ami	my boyfriend
ma petite amie	my girlfriend
mon jumeau	my twin (boy)
ma jumelle	my twin (girl)
mon fiancé	my fiancé
ma fiancée	my fiancée

la famille élargie	the extended family
ma grand-mère	my grandmother
ma mamie	my gran / grandma
mon grand-père	my grandfather
mon papi	my granddad
mes grands-parents	my grandparents
mon oncle	my uncle
ma tante	my aunt
mon cousin	my cousin (male)
ma cousine	my cousin (female)
mon neveu	my nephew
ma niece	my niece
mon petit-fils	my grandson
ma petite-fille	my granddaughter
mes petits-enfants	my grandchildren
mon beau-frère	my brother-in-law
ma belle-sœur	my sister-in-law
ma belle-mère	my mother-in-law
mon beau-père	my father-in-law
mes beaux-parents	my parents-in-law
mon gendre	my son-in-law
ma belle-fille	my daughter-in-law
ma belle-famille	my in-laws
mon arrière-grand-père	my great-grandfather
mon arrière-grand-mère	my great-grandmother
mes arrière-grands-parents	my great-grandparents
mon grand-oncle	my great-uncle

ma grand-tante	my great-aunt
mon arrière-petit-fils	my great-grandson
mon arrière-petite-fille	my great-granddaughter
my great-great-...	mon arrière-arrière...
mon filleul	my godson
ma filleule	my goddaughter
ma marraine	my godmother
mon parrain	my godfather

le bébé — the baby

un nouveau-né	a newborn (boy)
une nouveau-née	a newborn (girl)
un nourrisson	an infant
un tout-petit	a little one
un bambin	a toddler
un enfant	a child
un ado	a teenager
un adolescent(e)	an adolescent
un adulte	an adult

les amis	*the friends*
mon ami	my friend (male)
mon amie	my friend (female)
mon copain	my friend (male)
ma copine	my friend (female)
mon pote	my mate / buddy
mon poteau	my pal
mon meilleur ami	my best friend (male)
ma meilleure amie	my best friend (female)
être ami avec	to be friends with

Merci

Before you go, I'd like to say "merci" for buying this book. There are lots of French books available and you chose to read mine, so I am eternally grateful for that.

I hope you have enjoyed this book and I hope you're glad you made the purchase. I also hope you've started to realise how easy learning a new language can be.

This book contained course 5 (lessons thirty-six to forty-four) of my "3 Minute French" series. If you would like to learn more, you can get the next book in the series containing course 6, and further books after that to continue building your French language skills.

For more information on where to get the next books, or if you'd like any more tips on language learning, you can visit my website **http://www.3minute.club/**

You can also follow me on Twitter, Facebook or Instagram:

www.twitter.com/3mlanguages
www.facebook.com/3minutelanguages
www.instagram.com/3minutelanguages

You can get the video version of this and other 3 Minute French books by using the link below.

https://3minutelanguages.teachable.com/p/all-courses

Thank you again, merci et à bientôt!

Printed in Dunstable, United Kingdom